# UNITED METHODIST STUDIES

## Basic Bibliographies

*Fourth Edition*

Compiled and edited by

*KENNETH E. ROWE*

ABINGDON PRESS / Nashville

UNITED METHODIST STUDIES

98 99 00 01 02 03 04 05 06 07 — 10 9 8 7 6 5 4 3 2 1

MANUFACTURED IN THE UNITED STATES OF AMERICA

# PREFACE

These bibliographies have been compiled under the auspices of the United Methodist Studies Advisory Committee of the Division of Ordained Ministry of the General Board of Higher Education and Ministry of The United Methodist Church. They neither claim nor intend to provide exhaustive coverage of all areas of Methodist and Wesleyan scholarship. Their purpose is more modest: to provide a select list of the basic resources for students and instructors of seminary-level courses in United Methodist history, doctrine and polity, and to indicate minimum standards for libraries to support such courses.

In addition to standard texts, past and present, emphasis has been placed on selecting the best modern English language interpretations in print. Out-of-print works are included only if no suitable alternative exists. A few key journal articles are included in areas where there is no standard book-length treatment. Works not yet published as this guide goes to press are indicated as "forthcoming," and are included only if there is good reason to expect their timely publication under the titles given here.

The materials are arranged topically, and have been given item numbers for easy reference. An index of authors and editors is provided as an aid to locating works by particular individuals.

**Additions, corrections, and publications issued after December 1997, plus a large biographical section of British and American figures deleted from this edition, are available on the internet. Consult UMSTUDIES: BASIC BIBLIOGRAPHIES at www.gcah.org.**

Corrections and additions to, and deletions from, future editions of these bibliographies are welcomed and should be sent to the compiler: Kenneth E. Rowe, Librarian, Methodist Archives, Drew University, Madison, NJ 07940. Phone: 973-408-3910, FAX 973-408-3909, E-mail krowe@drew.edu.

**United Methodist Studies Advisory Committee 1996-2000**

Richard P. Heitzenrater, *Duke University Divinity School*
Robert H. Kohler, *Division of Ordained Ministry,*
*Section of Elders and Local Pastors*
Kenneth E. Rowe, *Drew University Theological School*
Theodore H. Runyon, *Candler School of Theology*
Jean Miller Schmidt, *Iliff School of Theology*

# CONTENTS

# PART VII: VIDEO RESOURCES

# PART I:
# BASIC LIBRARY FOR STUDENTS
# AND LOCAL CHURCHES

*A suggested reading list for seminary courses in United Methodist history, doctrine and polity, as well as a core library for local churches.*

## 1. The Basics

1001   *The Book of Discipline of The United Methodist Church*, 1996.
1002   *The Book of Resolutions of The United Methodist Church*, 1996.
1003   *The United Methodist Book of Worship*, 1992.
1004   *The United Methodist Hymnal*, 1989.
1005   *United Methodist Directory & Index of Resources.* Published annually.
1006   Rowe, Kenneth E. *United Methodist Studies: Basic Bibliographies.* 4th edition, 1998.

## 2. History
*For a full list of History resources, see Part III.*

1007   Heitzenrater, Richard P. *Wesley and the People Called Methodists.* Nashville: Abingdon Press, 1995.
1008   McEllhenney, John G., ed. *United Methodism in America: A Compact History.* Nashville: Abingdon Press, 1992.
1009   Richey, Russell E., Kenneth E. Rowe and Jean Miller Schmidt, eds. *Perspectives on American Methodism: Interpretive Essays.* Nashville: Kingswood Books, 1993.
1010   Schmidt, Jean Miller. *Grace Sufficient: A History of Women in American Methodism.* Nashville: Abingdon Press, 1999. Forthcoming.

*For local church libraries, add the following:*
1011   González, Justo L., ed. *Each in Our Own Tongue: A History of Hispanic United Methodism.* Nashville: Abingdon Press, 1991. Also available in Spanish: *En Nuestra Propria Lengua.*

1012 Guillermo, Artemio R., ed. *Churches Aflame: Asian Americans and United Methodism*. Nashville: Abingdon Press, 1991.
1013 Kirby, James E., Russell E. Richey and Kenneth E. Rowe. *The Methodists*. Westport, CT: Greenwood Press, 1996. (Denominations in America 8). Includes biographical dictionary and bibliographic essay.
1014 Noley, Homer. *First White Frost: Native Americans and United Methodism*. Nashville: Abingdon Press, 1991.
1015 Shockley, Grant S., ed. *Heritage and Hope: The African American Presence in United Methodism*. Nashville: Abingdon Press, 1991.

## 3. Doctrine
*For a full list of Doctrine resources, see Part IV.*

1016 Felton, Gayle C. *By Water and the Spirit: Making Connections for Identity and Ministry*. Nashville: Discipleship Resources, 1997. Full text of "By Water and the Spirit," statement on baptism adopted by General Conference 1996, with commentary.
1017 Langford, Thomas A., ed. *Doctrine and Theology in The United Methodist Church*. Nashville: Kingswood Books, 1990. Sets 1972 and 1988 UMC doctrinal statements in historical context.
1018 ———. *Practical Divinity*. Revised edition. Nashville: Abingdon Press, 1998. 2 vols. Vol. I, *Theology in the Wesleyan Tradition*, Vol. 2, *Readings In Wesleyan Theology*.
1019 Runyon, Theodore H. *The New Creation: John Wesley's Theology Today*. Nashville: Abingdon Press, 1998.
1020 Wesley, John. *John Wesley's Sermons, An Anthology*, edited by Albert C. Outler and Richard P. Heitzenrater. Nashville: Abingdon Press, 1991.

## 4. Polity
*For a full list of Polity resources, see Part V.*

1021 Frank, Thomas E. *Polity, Practice and Mission of The United Methodist Church*. Nashville: Abingdon Press, 1997.
1022 Tuell, Jack M. *The Organization of the United Methodist Church*. Revised 1997-2000 edition. Nashville: Abingdon Press, 1997.

## 5. Periodicals

*For a full list of Periodicals, see Part VI.*

1023   *Circuit Rider* (clergy journal)
1024   *Interpreter*; also available in Spanish: *El Intérprete,* and Korean: *United Methodist Family* (program journals)
1025   *Methodist History* (history journal)
1026   *Quarterly Review* (theology journal)
1027   *United Methodist Newscope* (weekly newsletter)
1028   *United Methodist Reporter,* national edition (weekly newspaper)

# PART II:
# GENERAL RESOURCES

## 1. Bibliographies
*For specialized bibliographies, see regional and topical subdivisions of Part III: History, and Part IV: Doctrine.*

2001  Calkin, Homer L. *Catalog of Methodist Archival and Manuscript Collections.* Alexandria, VA: World Methodist Historical Society, 1982-. Part 2: *Asia*, 1982. Part 3: *Australia and the South Pacific*, 1982. Part 6: *Great Britain and Ireland*, 1985-91.

2002  Harmon, Nolan B., ed. *Encyclopedia of World Methodism.* 2 vols. Nashville: United Methodist Publishing House, 1974. Bibliographies, 2:2721-2766.

2003  Rowe, Kenneth E., ed. *Methodist Union Catalog, Pre-1976 Imprints.* Lanham, MD: Scarecrow Press, 1975-. 7 volumes (A-Le) published to date.

2004  Vickers, John A. *Methodism and the Wesleys.* London: World Methodist Historical Society, 1987. Fifty key titles.

2005  Yrigoyen, Charles, Jr. and Susan E. Warrick. *Historical Dictionary of Methodism.* Lanham, MD: Scarecrow Press, 1996. Bibliography, 249-299.

## 2. Dictionaries/Handbooks

2006  Crosby, Pamela J. *Speaking Connectionally: How to Speak United Methodism.* Nashville: United Methodist Communications, 1991. A glossary of United Methodist terms, phrases, expressions, and acronyms.

2007  McAnally, Thomas S. *Questions and Answers about The United Methodist Church.* Nashville: Abingdon Press, 1995.

2008  Waltz, Alan K. *A Dictionary for United Methodists.* Nashville: Abingdon Press, 1991.

2009     Yrigoyen, Charles, Jr. and Susan E. Warrick, *Historical Dictionary of Methodism*. Lanham, MD: Scarecrow Press, 1996.

## 3. Directories

2010     *Archives and History Directory, 1997-2000*. Madison, NJ: General Commission on Archives & History, UMC, 1996.

2011     *General Minutes of the Annual Conferences of The United Methodist Church*. Chicago: General Council on Finance and Administration, UMC. Annual statistical review, clergy list, etc.

2012     *The United Methodist Directory and Index of Resources*. Edited by Gwen Colvin. Nashville: Cokesbury Press. Annual directory of bishops, councils, boards, commissions, conferences, news services and publications, schools, colleges and seminaries, study committees, caucuses, affiliated and ecumenical groups, programs, and resources. Also available from Cokesbury in electronic form.

2013     *World Methodist Council Handbook of Information, 1997-2002*. Lake Junaluska, NC: World Methodist Council, 1997. Directory of executive staff, committees, member churches, international dialogues, and statistics. Published quinquennially.

## 4. Encyclopedias

2014     Harmon, Nolan B., ed. *Encyclopedia of World Methodism*. 2 vols. Nashville: United Methodist Publishing House, 1974.

2015     McClintock, John, and James Strong. *Cyclopedia of Biblical, Theological and Ecclesiastical Literature*. 12 vols. New York: Arno Press, 1970. Reprint of the 1867-87 edition. Still standard for the 19th century.

2016     Simpson, Matthew. *Cyclopedia of Methodism*. New York: Gordon Press, 1977. Reprint of 1878 edition. Still standard for the 19th century.

# PART III:
# HISTORY

*For publications issued after December 1997, plus an extensive biography section for England and North America, consult UM Studies: Basic Bibliographies at www.gcah.org.*

## 1. Great Britain and Ireland

### A. Bibliographies
*See also General Bibliographies in Part II, Section 1.*

3001    Field, Clive D. *Anti-Methodist Publications of the Eighteenth Century: A Revised Bibliography.* Manchester: John Rylands University Library, 1991. Major revision and correction of Richard Green's 1902 bibliography of anti-Methodist publications.

3002    ———. "Bibliography of Methodist Historical Literature, 1974" (and succeeding years). Annual supplement to *Proceedings of the Wesley Historical Society* since June 1976.

3003    ———. "Bibliography." In *History of the Methodist Church in Great Britain*, 4:653-830. London: Epworth Press, 1988. The most comprehensive list of sources.

3004    ———. "Sources for the Study of Protestant Nonconformity in the John Rylands University Library of Manchester," *Bulletin of the John Rylands University Library of Manchester* 71/2 (Summer 1989): [103]-139. See especially the Methodist section, 121-135.

3005    Gage, Laurie E. *English Methodism: A Bibliographical View.* Westcliff-on-Sea, Essex: Gage Postal Books, 1985.

3006    Hatcher, Stephen. *A Primitive Methodist Bibliography.* Westcliff-on-Sea: Gage Postal Books, 1980.

3007    Turner, John Munsey. "British Methodist Historical Scholarship, 1893-1993: Wesley Historical Society Centenary," *Epworth Review* 20/3 (September 1993): 101-111.

3008    ———. "The Long Eighteenth Century: A Review Article," *Proceedings of the Wesley Historical Society* 51/1 (February 1997): 4-10.

## B. Surveys

3009   Davies, Rupert E. *Methodism*. 2nd revised edition. London: Epworth Press, 1985. Best survey.

3010   ———, and Gordon Rupp, eds. *A History of the Methodist Church in Great Britain*. 4 vols. London: Epworth Press, 1975- 1987. The basic work on all eras.

3011   Gilbert, Alan D. *Religion and Society in Industrial England: Church, Chapel and Social Change, 1740-1914*. London and New York: Longman, 1976.

3012   Hempton, David. *Methodism and Politics in British Society, 1750-1850*. Stanford: Stanford University Press, 1984.

3013   ———. *The Religion of the People: Methodism and Popular Religion, 1750-1900*. London: Routledge, 1996.

3014   Hylson-Smith, Kenneth. *The Churches in England from Elizabeth I to Elizabeth II*. 3 vols. London: SCM, 1997.

3015   McLeod, Hugh. *Religion and Society in England, 1850-1914*. New York: St. Martin's Press, 1996.

3016   Semmel, Bernard. *The Methodist Revolution*. New York: Basic Books, 1973.

3017   Swift, Wesley F. *Methodism in Scotland: The First Hundred Years*. London: Epworth Press, 1947.

3018   Tabraham, Barrie W. *The Making of Methodism*. London: Epworth Press, 1995. The best compact study.

3019   Taggart, Norman E. *The Irish in World Methodism, 1760-1900*. London: Epworth Press, 1986.

3020   Turner, John M. *Conflict and Reconciliation: Studies in Methodism and Ecumenism in England, 1740-1982*. London: Epworth Press, 1985.

## C. 18th Century Studies

*For biographies of John and Charles Wesley, and interpretations of their thought, see Part IV, Section 4.*

3021   Baker, Frank. *John Wesley and the Church of England*. Nashville: Parthenon Press, 1996. Reprint of the 1970 edition.

3022   Campbell, Ted. *The Religion of the Heart: A Study of European Religious Life in the Seventeenth and Eighteenth Centuries*. Columbia, SC: University of South Carolina Press, 1991. Sets the Methodist revival in larger context.

3023   Church, Leslie F. *The Early Methodist People*. London: Epworth Press, 1948.

3024   ———. *More About the Early Methodist People*. London: Epworth Press, 1949.

3025   Clark, Jonathan. *English Society 1688-1832: Ideology, Social Structure and Political Practice During the Ancien Régime.* Cambridge: Cambridge University Press, 1985.

3026    Dowley, T. E. *Through Wesley's England.* Nashville: Abingdon Press, 1988. Colorful guidebook to Wesley's England.

3027    Heitzenrater, Richard P. *Mirror and Memory: Reflections on Early Methodism.* Nashville: Kingswood Books, 1989.

3028    ———. *Wesley and the People Called Methodists.* Nashville: Abingdon Press, 1995. The basic work on Wesley and early Methodism.

3029    Olsen, Gerald W., ed. *Religion and Revolution in Early Industrial England: The Halevy Thesis and its Critics.* Lanham, MD: University Press of America, 1990.

3030    Rupp, Gordon. "Evangelical Revival." In his *Religion in England, 1688-1791.* Oxford: Clarendon Press, 1986, 326-490. Essential background and interpretation.

3031    Valentine, Simon Ross. *John Bennet and the Origins of Methodism and the Evangelcial Revival in England.* Lanham, MD: Scarecrow Press, 1997.

3032    Walsh, John D., et al., eds. *The Church of England, 1689-1833: From Toleration to Tractarianism.* Cambridge: Cambridge University Press, 1993. The best one-volume study of the whole century.

3033    Walsh, John D. "Methodism and the Origins of English-Speaking Evangelicalism." In *Evangelicalism: Comparative Studies of Popular Protestantism in North America, the British Isles, and Beyond,* edited by Mark Noll, et al. New York: Oxford University Press, 1994, 19-37.

3034    ———. "Origins of the Evangelical Revival." In *Essays in Modern English Church History,* edited by G. V. Bennett and J. D. Walsh. New York: Oxford University Press, 1966, 132-162.

3035    ———. "Religious Societies, Methodist and Evangelical, 1738-1800." In *Studies in Church History.* Oxford: Blackwell, 1986, 279-302.

3035.1  Ward, W. Reginald."The Eighteenth Century Church: A European View." In *The Church of England, 1689-1833,* edited by J. Walsh, et al.; see 3032, 185-298.

3036    ———. "The Evangelical Revival in Eighteenth Century Britain." In *History of Religion in Britain,* edited by S. Gilley and W. J. Sheils. Oxford : Blackwell, 1994, 252-274.

3037    ———. *Faith and Faction.* London: Epworth Press, 1993. Part 3: "Methodism."

3038    ———. *The Protestant Evangelical Awakening.* Cambridge: Cambridge University Press, 1992.

## D.  19th Century Studies

3039    Ambler, R. W. *Ranters, Revivalists & Reformers: Primitive Methodism and Rural Society, South Lincolnshire, 1817-1875*. Hull: Hull University Press, 1989.

3040 Carwardine, Richard. *Trans-Atlantic Revivalism: Popular Evangelicalism in Britain and America, 1790-1865*. Westport, CT: Greenwood Press, 1978.

3041 Currie, Robert. *Methodism Divided: A Study in the Sociology of Ecumenicalism*. London: Faber, 1968. Details divisions and reunions of the Methodist family in England after Wesley.

3042 Hempton, David. "The Methodists." In *Nineteenth-Century English Religious Traditions: Retrospect and Prospects*, edited by D.G.Paz. Westport, CT: Greenwood Press, 1995, 117-141.

3043 Kent, John. *The Age of Disunity*. London: Epworth Press, 1966.

3044 ———. *Holding the Fort: Studies in Victorian Revivalism*. London: Epworth Press, 1978.

3045 Moore, Robert. *Pit-Men, Preachers & Politics: The Effects of Methodism in a Durham Mining Community*. Cambridge: Cambridge University Press, 1974.

3046 Nockles, Peter. *The Oxford Movement in Context: Anglican High Churchmanship, 1760-1857*. Cambridge: Cambridge University Press, 1994.

3047 Rose, E. Alan. "The Methodist New Connexion, 1797-1907," *Proceedings of the Wesley Historical Society* 47/6 (October 1980): 241-253.

3048 Selen, Mats. *The Oxford Movement and Wesleyan Methodism in England: 1833-1882*. Lund, Sweden: Lund University Press, 1992.

3049 Thompson, E. P. *The Making of the English Working Class*. London: Penguin, 1968.

3050 Watts, Michael R. *The Dissenters, Vol. II: The Expansion of Evangelical Nonconformity [1791-1869]*. Oxford: Clarendon Press, 1995.

3051 Wearmouth, Robert F. *Methodism and the Working-Class Movements in England, 1800-1850*. Clifton, NJ: Augustus M. Kelley Publishers, 1972. Reprint of 1937 edition.

3052 Werner, Julia S. *The Primitive Methodist Connexion: Its Background and Early History*. Madison, WI: University of Wisconsin Press, 1984.

## E. 20th Century Studies

3053 Brake, G. Thompson. *Policy and Politics in British Methodism, 1932-1982*. London: B. Edsall & Co., Ltd., 1985.

3054 Davies, Rupert E. *The Testing of the Churches, 1932-1982: A Symposium*. London: Epworth Press, 1982.

3055 Turner, John Munsey. *Modern Methodism in England, 1932-1996*. London: Epworth Press, 1997.

## 2. North America

### A. Bibliographies

*See also General Bibliographies in Part II, Section 1.*

3056  Bucke, Emory S., ed. *History of American Methodism.* 3 vols. Nashville: Abingdon Press, 1964. See bibliographies at the end of each volume.

3057  Rowe, Kenneth E. "Methodist History at the Bicentennial." *Methodist History* 22 (1984): 87-98.

### B. Surveys

3058  Airhart, Phyllis. *Serving the Present Age: Revivialism, Progressivism and the Methodist Tradition in Canada.* Kingston, Ontario: McGill-Queens University Press, 1992.

3059  Bucke, Emory S., ed. *History of American Methodism.* 3 vols. Nashville: Abingdon Press, 1974.

3060  Curts, Lewis. *The General Conferences of the Methodist Episcopal Church from 1792 to 1896.* Cincinnati: Curts & Jennings; New York: Eaton & Mains, 1900. Useful outline history of MEC General Conferences through 1896.

3061  Kirby, James E., Russell E. Richey and Kenneth E. Rowe. *The Methodists.* Westport, CT: Greenwood Press, 1996.

3062  Lawrence, William B., et al, eds. *The People(s) Called Methodist: Forms and Reforms of Their Life.* Nashville: Abingdon Press, 1997. (United Methodism and American Culture series.)

3063  McEllhenney, John G., ed. *United Methodism in America: A Compact History.* Nashville: Abingdon Press, 1992. The best brief study.

3064  Norwood, Frederick A. *The Story of American Methodism: A History of the United Methodists and Their Relations.* Nashville: Abingdon Press, 1974.

3065  ———, ed. *Sourcebook of American Methodism.* Nashville: Parthenon Press, 1996. Reprint of the 1983 edition.

3066  Richey, Russell E. "History as a Bearer of Denominational Identity: Methodism as a Case Study." Reprinted in *Perspectives on American Methodism,* chapter 32, 480-498; see 3070.

3067  ———. *The Methodist Conference in America: A History.* Nashville: Kingswood Books, 1996.

3068  Richey, Russell E., Dennis M. Campbell and William B. Lawrence, eds. *United Methodism and American Culture.* Nashville: Abingdon Press, 1997. Vol. 1: *Connectionalism: Ecclesiology, Mission, and Identity*; vol. 2: *The People(s) Called Methodists: Forms and Reforms of Their Life.*

3069  ——— and Kenneth E. Rowe, eds. *Rethinking Methodist History.* Nashville: Kingswood Books, 1985.

3070 ———, Kenneth E. Rowe, and Jean Miller Schmidt, eds. *Perspectives on American Methodism: Interpretive Essays*. Nashville: Kingswood Books, 1993.

3071 Semple, Neil. *The Lord's Dominion: The History of Canadian Methodism*. Montreal: McGill-Queen's University Press, 1996.

3072 Sweet, William W., ed. *Religion on the American Frontier, 1783-1940: The Methodists, A Collection of Source Materials*. New York: Cooper Square, 1964. Reprint of 1946 edition.

3073 *Timelines of United Methodist History, 1703-1996*. Madison, NJ: General Commission on Archives and History, UMC, 1996.

## C. 18th Century Studies

3074 Andrews, Dee. "Religion and Social Change: The Rise of the Methodists." In *Shaping a National Culture: The Philadelphia Experience, 1750-1800*. Winterthur, DE: Henry Francis du Pont Winterthur Museum, 1994, 143-168.

3075 Baker, Frank. *From Wesley to Asbury: Studies in Early American Methodism*. Durham, NC: Duke University Press, 1976.

3076 Lee, Jesse. *A Short History of the Methodists*. Rutland, VT: Academy Books, 1974. Reprint of the first published history of Methodism in America, 1810.

3077 Richey, Russell E. *Early American Methodism*. Bloomington, IN: Indiana University Press, 1991.

3078 Williams, William H. "The Attraction of Methodism: The Delmarva Peninsula as a Case Study, 1769-1820." Reprinted in *Perspectives on American Methodism*, chapter 2, 31-45; see 3070.

3079 ———. *The Garden of Methodism: The Delmarva Peninsula, 1769-1820*. Wilmington, DE: Scholarly Resources Inc., 1984.

## D. 19th Century Studies

3080 Bilhartz, Terry D. *Urban Religion and the Second Great Awakening: Church and Society in Early National Baltimore*. Rutherford, NJ: Fairleigh Dickinson University Press, 1986.

3081 Carwardine, Richard J. *Evangelicals and Politics in Antebellum America*. New Haven: Yale University Press, 1993.

3082 ———. *Transatlantic Revivalism: Popular Evangelicalism in Britain and America, 1790-1865*. Westport, CT: Greenwood Press, 1978.

3083 Goen, Charles C. *Broken Churches, Broken Nation: Denominational Schism and the Coming of the Civil War*. Macon, GA: Mercer University Press, 1985.

3084 Jones, Donald G. *The Sectional Crisis and Northern Methodism: A Study in Piety, Political Ethics, and Civil Religion*. Metuchen, NJ: Scarecrow Press, 1979.

3085 Marti, Donald B. "Rich Methodists": The Rise and Consequences of Lay Philanthropy in the Mid-Nineteenth Century." Reprinted in *Perspectives on American Methodism*, chapter 16, 265-176; see 3070.

3086 Mathews, Donald G. "Evangelical America—The Methodist Ideology." Reprinted in *Perspectives on American Methodism*, chapter 1, 17-30; see 3070.

3087 ———. *Religion in the Old South*. Chicago: University of Chicago Press, 1977.

3088 Schneider, A. Gregory. "Social Religion, the Christian Home, and Republican Spirituality in Antebellum Methodism." Reprinted in *Perspectives on American Methodism*, chapter 12, 192-208; see 3070.

3089 ———. *The Way of the Cross Leads Home: The Domestication of American Methodism*. Bloomington, IN: Indiana University Press, 1993.

3090 Strong, Douglas M. *Perfectionist Politics: Ecclesiastical Abolitionism and the Tensions of American Democracy*. Syracuse, NY: Syracuse University Press, 1997.

## E. 20th Century Studies

3091 Gorrell, Donald K. *The Age of Social Responsibility: The Social Gospel in the Progressive Era 1900-1920*. Macon, GA: Mercer University Press, 1988.

3092 Messer, Donald E. and William J. Abraham, eds. *Unity, Liberty and Charity: Building Bridges Under Icy Waters*. Nashville: Abingdon Press, 1996.

3093 Moore, John N. *The Long Road to Methodist Union*. Nashville: Methodist Publishing House, 1943.

3094 Muelder, Walter G. *Methodism and Society in the Twentieth Century*. Nashville: Abingdon Press, 1961.

3095 Sledge, Robert Watson. *Hands on the Ark: The Struggle for Change in the Methodist Episcopal Church, South, 1914-1939*. Lake Junaluska, NC: General Commission on Archives and History, UMC, 1975.

3096 Straughn, James Henry. *Inside Methodist Union*. Nashville : Methodist Publishing House, 1958.

3097 Washburn, Paul. *An Unfinished Church: A Brief History of the Union of the Evangelical United Brethren Church and The Methodist Church*. Nashville: Abingdon Press, 1985.

## 3. Africa

3098 Bartels, Francis L. *The Roots of Ghana Methodism*. Cambridge: Cambridge University Press, 1965.

3099 Calhoun, Eugene Clayton. *Of Men Who Ventured Much and Far: Dr. Gilbert and Bishop Lambuth*. Atlanta: The Institute Press, 1961.

3100 Campbell, James T. *Songs of Zion: The African Methodist Episcopal Church in the United States and South Africa*. New York: Oxford University Press, 1995.

3101 Coan, Josephus R. *Flying Sparks: The Genesis of African Methodism in South Africa*. Nashville: AMEC Publishing House, 1987.

3102 Cochrane, James R. "Servants of Power: The Role of English-speaking Churches in South Africa, 1903-1930." In *Toward a Critical Theology via an Historical Analysis of the Anglican and Methodist Churches*. Johannesburg: Ravan Press, 1987.

3103 Garrett, A. E. F. *South African Methodism: Her Missionary Witness*. Cape Town, South Africa: Methodist Publishing House, 1965.

3104 Johnson, Walton R. *Worship and Freedom: A Black American Church in Zambia*. New York: Africana Publishing Co., 1977.

3105 Kasongo, Michael. *History of the Methodist Church in the Central Congo, 1912-1997*. Lanham, MD: University Press of America, 1998.

3106 Kurewa, John Wesley Z. *The Church in Mission: A Short History of The United Methodist Church in Zimbabwe, 1897-1997*. Nashville: Abingdon Press, 1997.

3107 Mears, W. Gordon. *Methodism in the Cape: An Outline*. Cape Town, South Africa: Methodist Publishing House, 1973.

3108 Muzorewa, Abel T. *Rise Up and Walk: The Autobiography of Bishop Abel T. Muzorewa*. Edited by Norman E. Thomas. Nashville: Abingdon Press, 1978.

3109 Oosthuizen, G. C., et al, eds. *Afro-Christianity at the Grassroots: Its Dynamics and Strategies*. Leiden: E. J. Brill, 1994.

3110 Reid, Alexander J. *Congo Drumbeat: History of the First Half Century in the Establishment of the Methodist Church among the Atetela of Central Congo*. New York: World Outlook Press, 1964.

3111 Shank, David A. *Prophet Harris, the 'Black Elijah' of West Africa*. Leiden: E. J. Brill, 1994.

## 4. Asia and the Pacific

3112 Alejandro, Dionisio Deista. *From Darkness To Light: A Brief Chronicle of the Beginnings and Spread of Methodism in the Philippines*. Quezon City, Philippines: The United Methodist Church, Philippines Central Conference, Board of Communications and Publications, 1974.

3113 Baker, Richard T. *Ten Thousand Years: The Story of Methodism's First*

*Century in China.* New York: Board of Missions of The Methodist Church, 1947.

3114 Colwell, James. *The Illustrated History of Methodism: Australia, New South Wales, and Polynesia.* Sydney: W. Brooks, 1904.

3115 Deats, Richard L. *The Story of Methodism in the Philippines.* Manila: Union Theological Seminary, 1964.

3116 Forman, Charles. *The Island Churches of the South Pacific: Emergence in the Twentieth Century.* Maryknoll: Orbis Books, 1982.

3117 Garrett, John. *To Live among the Stars: Christian Origins in Oceania.* Geneva: World Council of Churches in association with the Institute of Pacific Studies, University of the South Pacific, 1982.

3118 ———. *Footsteps in the Sea: Christianity in Oceania to World War II.* Geneva: World Council of Churches in association with the Institute of Pacific Studies, Universty of the South Pacific, 1992.

3119 Grayson, James H. *Korea: A Religious History.* New York: Oxford University Press, 1989.

3120 Harper, Marvin H. *The Methodist Episcopal Church in India.* Lucknow: Lucknow Publishing House, 1936.

3121 Hollister, John N. *The Centenary of the Methodist Church in Southern Asia.* Lucknow: Lucknow Publishing House, 1956.

3122 Krummel, John W. *The Methodist Protestant Church in Japan.* 2 parts. Tokyo: Aoyama Gakuin University, 1982-1983.

3123 Lacy, Walter N. *A Hundred Years of China Methodism.* Nashville: Abingdon-Cokesbury, 1948.

3124 Latukefu, Sione. *Church and State in Tonga: The Wesleyan Methodist Missionaries and Political Development, 1822-1875.* Honolulu: University Press of Hawaii, 1974.

3125 Piggin, Stuart. *Evangelical Christianity in Australia: Spirit, Word and World.* Melbourne: Oxford University Press, 1996.

3126 Robledo, Liwliwa T. *Gender, Religion and Social Change: A Study of Philippine Methodist Deaconesses, 1903-1978.* Doctoral dissertation, Iliff School of Theology/University of Denver, 1996.

3127 Senior, Geoffrey R. *The China Experience: A Study of the Methodist Mission in China.* Peterborough, England: WMHS Publications, 1994.

3128 Shin-Lee, Kyung-Lim. "Sisters in Christ: American Women Missionaries in Ewha Women's University." In *Spirituality and Social Responsibility.* Edited by Rosemary Skinner Keller. Nashville: Abingdon Press, 1993, 185-203.

3129 *Waves, 1888-1988: The United Methodist Church of Hawaii: A Centennial Jubilee.* Edited by Alex R. Vergara. Koloa, Hawaii: Taylor Publishing of Kauai; Honolulu: United Methodist Union, 1988.

# 5. Central and South America

3130    Bruno-Jofre, Rosa del Carmen. *Methodist Education in Peru: Social Gospel, Politics, and American Ideological and Economic Penetration, 1888-1930*. Waterloo, ONT: Wilfrid Laurier University Press, 1988.

3131    Dussel, Enrique, ed. *The Church in Latin America, 1492-1992*. Turnbridge Wells, England: Burns & Oates; Maryknoll, NY: Orbis Books, 1992.

3132    *For Ever Beginning: Two Hundred Years of Methodism in the Western Area*. Kingston, Jamaica: Literature Department of the Methodist Church, Jamaica District, 1960.

3133    González, Justo L. *The Development of Christianity in the Latin Caribbean*. Grand Rapids, MI: Wm. B. Eerdmans, 1969.

3134    *Kindling of the Flame: How the Methodist Church Expanded in the Caribbean*. Demerara, British Guiana: Published for the Methodist Centenary Celebrations in the Western Area by the British Guiana District, 1960.

3135    Kirkpatrick, Dow, ed. *Faith Born in the Struggle for Life: A Re-reading of Protestant Faith in Latin America Today*. Grand Rapids, MI: Wm. B. Eerdmans, 1988.

3136    Martin, David. *Tongues of Fire: The Explosion of Protestantism in Latin America*. Oxford, UK, and Cambridge, MA: B. Blackwell, 1990.

3137    Míguez Bonino, José. *Faces of Latin American Protestantism*. Grand Rapids, MI: Wm. B. Eerdmans, 1997.

3138    Neblett, Sterling A. *Methodism's First Fifty Years in Cuba*. Macon, GA: Wesleyan College, 1966.

3139    Porter, Eugene Oliver. *A History of Methodism in Mexico*. Doctoral dissertation, Ohio State University, 1939.

# 6. Europe

3140    Hagen, Odd. *Preludes to Methodism in Northern Europe*. Oslo: Norsk Forlagsselskap, 1961.

3141    Istomina, Lydia. *Bringing Hidden Things to Light: The Revival of Methodism in Russia*. Nashville: Abingdon Press, 1997.

3142    Kimbrough, S. T., Jr., ed. *Methodism in Russia & the Baltic States: History and Revewal*. Nashville: Kingswood Books, 1996.

3143    Kissack, Reginald. *Methodists in Italy*. London: Cargate Press, 1960.

3144    Ludlow, Peter W. *The Churches in the European Union*. London:

Methodist Church Division of Social Responsibility, 1994. (Beckly Social Service Lecture 1994)

3145 Marquardt, Manfred. "Adaptation or Resistance: Christian Churches in Germany and their Policies under Totalitarian Regimes," *Quarterly Review* 15/1 (Spring 1995): 23-69.

3146 Nauser, Wilhelm. *Be Eager to Maintain the Unity of the Spirit Through the Bond of Peace, A Short History of the Geneva Area of The United Methodist Church.* Cincinnati: General Board of Global Ministries, UMC, 1985.

3147 Ramet, Sabrina P., ed. *Protestantism and Politics in Eastern Europe and Russia: Communist and Postcommunist Eras.* Durham, NC: Duke University Press, 1992.

3148 Short, Roy H. *History of Methodism in Europe.* Nashville: Office of the Secretary of the Council of Bishops, UMC, 1980.

3149 Stephens, Peter. *Methodism in Europe.* Cincinnati: General Board of Global Ministries, UMC, 1981.

3150 *Under One Roof: The UK and Europe in the 21st Century.* London: Methodist Church Division of Social Responsibility, 1993.

3151 Wardin, Albert W., Jr. *Evangelical Sectarianism in the Russian Empire and the USSR: A Bibliographical Guide.* Metuchen, NJ: Scarecrow Press, 1995.

## 7. African American Methodists

3152 Andrews, Dee. "The African Methodists of Philadelphia, 1794-1802." *Pennsylvania Magazine of History and Biography* 108 (October 1984): 471-486. Reprinted in *Perspectives on American Methodism*, chapter 9, 145-158; see 3070.

3153 Baldwin, Lewis V. *"Invisible" Strands in African Methodism: A History of the African Union Methodist Protestant and Union American Methodist Episcopal Churches, 1805-1980.* Metuchen, NJ: Scarecrow Press, 1983.

3154 Bradley, David H. *A History of the A.M.E. Zion Church, 1796-1968.* 2 vols. Nashville: A.M.E. Zion Publishing House, 1956-1960.

3155 Culver, Dwight W. *Negro Segregation in the Methodist Church.* New Haven: Yale University Press, 1953.

3156 Daniels, George M. *Turning Corners: Reflections of African Americans in The United Methodist Church from 1961 to 1993.* Dayton, OH: General Council on Ministries, UMC, 1997.

3157 Dickerson, Dennis C. *Religion, Race, and Region: Research Notes on A.M.E. Church History.* Nashville: Legacy Publishing, 1995.

3158 Dvorak, Katherine L. *An African-American Exodus: The Segregation of the Southern Churches.* Brooklyn, NY: Carlson Publishing Inc., 1991.

3159 George, Carol V. R. *Segregated Sabbaths: Richard Allen and the Rise of the Independent Black Churches, 1760-1840.* New York: Oxford University Press, 1973.

3160 Gravely, Will B. "African Methodisms and the Rise of Black Denominationalism." Reprinted in *Perspectives on American Methodism*, chapter 7, 108-126; see 3070.

3161 ———. "The Rise of African Churches in America: Re-examining the Contexts, 1786-1822." In *African American Religious Studies*, edited by G. S. Wilmore. Durham, NC: Duke University Press, 1989, 301-317.

3162 Gray, C. Jarrett, Jr., comp. *The Racial and Ethnic Presence in American Methodism: A Bibliography.* Madison, NJ: General Commission on Archives and History, UMC, 1991.

3163 Gregg, Howard D. *History of the African Methodist Episcopal Church: The Black Church in Action.* Nashville: A.M.E. Church Sunday School Union, 1980.

3164 Hildebrand, Reginald F., *The Times Were Strange and Stirring: Methodist Preachers and the Crisis of Emancipation.* Durham, NC: Duke University Press, 1995.

3165 Jones, Donald G. *The Sectional Crisis and Northern Methodism: A Study in Piety, Political Ethics and Civil Religion.* Metuchen, NJ: Scarecrow Press, 1979.

3166 Lakey, Othal L. *God in My Mamma's House: A Study of the Women's Movement in the C.M.E. Church.* Memphis, TN: C.M.E. Publishing House, 1994.

3167 ———. *The History of the C.M.E. Church.* Revised edition. Memphis, TN: The C.M.E. Publishing House, 1996.

3168 McClain, William B. *Black People in the Methodist Church: Whither Thou Goest?* Nashville: Abingdon Press, 1984.

3169 McKay, Nellie Y. "Nineteenth-Century Black Women's Spiritual Autobiographies: Religious Faith and Self-Empowerment." Reprinted in *Perspectives on American Methodism*, chapter 11, 178-191; see 3070.

3170 Mathews, Donald G. *Slavery and Methodism: A Chapter in American Morality, 1780-1845.* Westport, CT: Greenwood Press, 1978. Reprint of the 1965 edition.

3171 ———. *Religion in the Old South.* Chicago: University of Chicago Press, 1977.

3172 Montgomery, William E. *Under Their Own Vine and Fig Tree: The African-American Church in the South, 1865-1900.* Baton Rouge, LA: Louisiana University Press, 1993.

3173 Morrow, Ralph E. *Northern Methodism and Reconstruction.* East Lansing, MI: Michigan State University Press, 1956.

3174  Murray, Peter C. *Christ and Caste in Conflict: Creating a Racially Inclusive Methodist Church*. Doctoral dissertation, Indiana University, 1985.

3175  Nash, Gary B. *Forging Freedom: The Formation of Philadelphia's Black Community, 1720-1840*. Cambridge: Harvard University Press, 1988. See especially chapter 4.

3176  Raboteau, Albert J. *Fire in the Bones: Reflections on African-American Religious History*. Boston: Beacon Press, 1995. See especially chapter 4, "Richard Allen and the African Church Movement."

3177  Richardson, Harry V. *Dark Salvation: The Story of Methodism as it Developed among Blacks in America*. New York: Doubleday, 1976.

3178  Shockley, Grant S., ed. *Heritage and Hope: The African American Presence in United Methodism*. Nashville: Abingdon Press, 1991. The basic work.

3179  Smith, Warren T. *Harry Hosier, Circuit Rider*. Nashville: Discipleship Resources, 1994.

3180  ———. *John Wesley and Slavery*. Nashville: Abingdon Press, 1986. Includes facsimile reprint of Wesley's important "Thoughts Upon Slavery."

3181  Thomas, James S. *Methodism's Racial Dilemma: The Story of the Central Jurisdiction*. Nashville: Abingdon Press, 1992.

3182  Walker, Clarence E. *A Rock in a Weary Land: The African Methodist Episcopal Church During the Civil War and Reconstruction*. Baton Rouge, LA : Louisiana State University Press, 1982.

3183  Walls, William J. *The African Methodist Episcopal Zion Church*. Charlotte, NC : A.M.E. Zion Publishing House, 1974.

3184  Williams, Gilbert A. *The Christian Recorder, Newspaper of the African Methodist Episcopal Church: History of a Forum for Ideas, 1854-1902*. Jefferson, NC: McFarland, 1997.

## 8. Asian American Methodists
*See also Part III, Section 4: Asia and the Pacific.*

3185  Barclay, Wade C. *History of Methodist Missions*. 4 vols. New York: Board of Missions, The Methodist Church, 1949-1957. See especially 3:286-296.

3186  *The Burning Heart: Visions for Asian-American Missional Congregations*. New York: National Program Division, General Board of Global Ministries, UMC, 1990.

3187  Chai, Alice. "Korean Women in Hawaii, 1903-1945: The Role of Methodism in their Liberation and in their Participation in the Korean Independence Movement." In *Women in New Worlds*. Nashville: Abingdon Press, 1981, I: 328-344.

3188    Choy, Bong-Youn. *Koreans in America*. Chicago: Nelson-Hall, 1979. See especially chapter 13, "Korean Religious and Cultural Activities."

3189    Gibson, Otis. *The Chinese in America*. New York: Arno Press, 1978. Reprint of 1877 edition.

3190    Gray, C. Jarrett, Jr., comp. *The Racial and Ethnic Presence in American Methodism: A Bibliography*. Madison, NJ: General Commission on Archives and History, UMC, 1991.

3191    Guillermo, Artemio R., ed. *Churches Aflame: Asian Americans and United Methodism*. Nashville: Abingdon Press, 1991. The basic work.

3192    Hurh, Wom Moo. *The Korean Immigrants in America*. Cranbury, NJ: Associated University Press, 1984.

3193    Kim, Ai Ra. *Women Struggling for a New Life: The Role of Religion in the Cultural Passage from Korea to America*. Albany, NY: State University of New York Press, 1996.

3194    Kim, Byong-suh, and Sang Hyun Lee, eds. *The Korean Immigrant in America*. New Jersey: Association of Korean Christian Scholars in North America, 1980.

3195    Kim, Helen. *Grace Sufficient: The Story of Helen Kim*. Nashville: Upper Room, 1964.

3196    Kim, Hyung-chan. *The Korean Diaspora*. Santa Rosa, CA: Clio Publications, 1977. See especially "History and Role of the Church in the Korean American Community," 47-64.

3197    Kim, Illsoo. *New Urban Immigrants: The Korean Community in New York*. Princeton, NJ: Princeton University Press, 1981. Includes major section on the churches.

3198    ———. "Organizational Patterns of Korean-American Methodist Churches: Denominationalism and Personal Community." In *Rethinking Methodist History*, edited by Russell E. Richey and Kenneth E. Rowe, 228-238; see 3069.

3199    Kim, Jung Ha, *Bridge-Makers and Cross-Bearers: Korean American Women and the Church*. Atlanta: Scholars Press, 1995.

3200    Koga, Sumio, comp. *A Centennial Legacy: History of the Japanese Christian Missions in North America*. Chicago: Nobart Inc., 1977.

3201    Matsuoka, Fumitaka, *Out of Silence: Emerging Themes in Asian American Churches*. Cleveland : United Church Press, 1995

3202    Suzuki, Lester E. *Ministry in the Assembly and Relocation Centers of World War II*. Berkeley, CA: Yardbird Publishing Co., 1979.

3203    Takaki, Ronald. *Strangers from a Different Shore: A History of Asian Americans*. Boston: Little, Brown, 1989. Gives essential background and describes the larger context.

3204    Woo, Wesley S. *Protestant Work among the Chinese in the San Francisco*

*Bay Area, 1850-1920.* Doctoral dissertation, Graduate Theological Union, 1984.

## 9. Camp Meetings
*See also Part III, Section 23: Holiness Movement.*

3205 Acornley, John H. *A History of the Primitive Methodist Church in the United States of America.* Fall River, NW: Matthews, 1909.

3206 Brown, Kenneth O. *Holy Ground: A Study of the American Camp Meeting.* New York: Garland, 1992.

3207 Bruce, Dickson D. *And They All Sang Hallelujah: Plain-Folk Camp-Meeting Religion, 1800-1845.* Knoxville, TN: University of Tennessee Press, 1974.

3208 Hughes, George. *Days of Power in the Forest Temple: A Review of the Wonderful Work of God at Fourteeen National Camp- Meetings from 1867 to 1872.* Salem, OH: Allegheny Wesleyan Methodist Connection, 1975. Reprint of the 1873 edition.

3209 Johnson, Charles A. *The Frontier Camp Meeting: Religion's Harvest Time.* With a new introduction by Ferenc M. Szasz. Dallas, TX: Southern Methodist University Press, 1985.

3210 McLean, A. and J. W. Eaton. *Penuel; or, Face to Face With God.* New York: Garland, 1984. Reprint of 1869 edition.

3211 Parnes, Brenda. "Ocean Grove: A Planned Leisure Environment." In *Planned and Utopian Experiments, Four New Jersey Towns,* edited by Paul A. Stellhorn. Trenton, NJ: New Jersey Historical Commission, 1980, 28-47.

3212 Uminowicz, Glenn. "Recreation in America: Ocean Grove and Asbury Park, New Jersey, 1869-1914." In *Hard At Play: Leisure in America, 1840-1940.* Edited by Kathryn Grover. Amherst, MA: University of Massachusetts Press, 1992, 8-38.

3213 Weiss, Ellen B. *City in the Woods: The Life and Design of an American Camp Meeting on Martha's Vineyard.* New York: Oxford University Press, 1987.

3214 Wilkes, Arthur. *Mow Cop and the Camp Meeting Movement: Sketches of Primitive Methodism.* Leominster, England: Orphans' Printing Press, 1942.

## 10. Chaplains

3215 Boozer, Jack S. *Edge of Ministry, the Chaplain Story: The Chaplain Ministry of The United Methodist Church, 1945-1980.* Nashville: General Board of Higher Education and Ministry, UMC, 1984.

## 11. Charismatic/Pentecostal Movement
*See also Part III, Section 5: Central and South America.*

3216   Bartleman, Frank. *Witness to Pentecost: The Life of Frank Bartleman*. Edited by Cecil M. Robeck, Jr. New York: Garland, 1985. Reprints four autobiographical tracts with introduction notes and commentary.

3217   Davison, Leslie. *Pathway to Power: The Charismatic Movement in Historical Perspective*. Watchung, NJ: Logos Books, 1972.

3218   Dayton, Donald W. *The Theological Roots of Pentecostalism*. Grand Rapids, MI: Francis Asbury Press of Zondervan Publishing House, 1987.

3219   Greet, Kenneth. *When the Spirit Moves*. London: Epworth Press, 1975.

3220   *Guidelines: The United Methodist Church and the Charismatic Renewal*. Nashville: Discipleship Resources, 1976. A statement approved by the 1976 General Conference.

3221   Jones, Charles Edwin. *Black Holiness: A Guide to the Study of Black Participation in Wesleyan Perfectionist and Glossalalic Pentecostal Movements*. Metuchen, NJ: Scarecrow Press, 1987.

3222   ———. *A Guide to the Study of the Pentecostal Movement*. 2 vols. Metuchen, NJ: Scarecrow Press, 1983.

3223   ———. *The Charismatic Movement: A Guide to the Study of Neo-Pentecostalism, with Emphasis on Anglo-American Sources*. Metuchen, NJ: Scarecrow Press, 1995.

3224   McDonnell, Kilian, ed. *Presence, Power, Praise: Documents on the Charismatic Renewal*. 3 vols. Collegeville, MN: Liturgical Press, 1980. Contains full texts of the official resolutions and study documents of Methodist Churches in Australia, England, and the United States.

3225   Robb, Edmund W. *The Spirit Who Will Not Be Tamed: The Wesleyan Message and the Charismatic Experience*. Anderson, IN: Bristol Books, 1997.

3226   Snyder, Howard A., with Daniel V. Runyon. *The Divided Flame: Wesleyans and the Charismatic Renewal*. Grand Rapids, MI: Francis Asbury Press of Zondervan Publishing House, 1986.

3227   Stokes, Mack B. *The Holy Spirit in the Wesleyan Heritage*. Nashville: Graded Press, 1985.

3228   Synan, Vinson. *The Holiness-Pentecostal Tradition: Charismatic Movements in the Twentieth Century*. Revised & enlarged edition. Grand Rapids, MI: Wm. B. Eerdmans, 1997.

3229   Tuttle, Robert G., Jr. "Can United Methodists Be Charismatics?" *Circuit Rider* 2/6 (April 1978): 3-6.

3230   Wesley, John. "Cautions and Directions Given to the Greatest Professors in the Methodist Societies" (1762). In *John Wesley*, edited by Albert C. Outler, 298-305; see 4050.

3231 ———. "The Nature of Enthusiasm" (1750). Sermon 37 in *The Works of John Wesley, Bicentennial Edition*, 2:44-60.

3232 ———. "The Witness of the Spirit, Discourses I and II" (1746 and 1767). Sermons 10-11 in *The Works of John Wesley, Bicentennial Edition*, 1:267-298.

## 12. Christian Education

3233 Bowen, Cawthon A. *Child and Church: A History of Methodist Church School Curriculum*. New York: Abingdon, 1960.

3234 Boylan, Ann M. *Sunday School: The Formation of an American Institution*. New Haven: Yale University Press, 1988.

3235 *Foundations: Shaping the Ministry of Education in Your Congregation*. Nashville: Discipleship Resources, 1993. Training guide and planning set; available in Spanish and Korean.

3236 Morrison, Theodore. *Chautauqua: A Center for Education, Religion, and the Arts in America*. Chicago: University of Chicago Press, 1974.

3237 Rowe, Kenneth E. "Members." Part 3, *The Methodists* by James E. Kirby, Russell E. Richey, and Kenneth E. Rowe. Westport, CT: Greenwood Press, 1996, 165-254.

3238 Sangster, Paul. *Pity My Simplicity: The Evangelical Revival and the Religious Education of Children, 1738-1800*. London: Epworth Press, 1963.

3239 Schisler, John Q. *Christian Education in Local Methodist Churches*. Nashville: Abingdon Press, 1969. The basic history.

3240 Seymour, Jack. *From Sunday School to Church School: Continuities in Protestant Christian Education in the U.S., 1860-1929*. Washington, DC: University Press of America, 1982.

3241 Shockley, Grant S. and Ethel R. Johnson. *The Christian Education Journey of Black Americans*. Nashville: Discipleship Resources, 1985.

## 13. Church Architecture

3242 Dolby, George W. *The Architectural Expression of Methodism: The First Hundred Years*. London: Epworth Press, 1964. Discusses England only.

3243 Garber, Paul Neff. *The Methodist Meeting House*. New York: Board of Missions and Church Extension, The Methodist Church, 1941.

3244 Jobson, Frederick J. *Chapel and School Architecture*. Peterborough, England: Methodist Publishing House, 1991. Reprint of the 1850 edition.

3245 Kilde, Jeanne Halgren. *Spiritual Armories: A Social and Architectural*

*History of Neo-Medieval Auditorium Churches in the U.S., 1869-1910.* Doctoral dissertation, University of Minnesota, 1991.

3246 Rowe, Kenneth E. "Redesigning Methodist Churches: Auditorium-style Sanctuaries and Akron-Plan Sunday Schools in Romanesque Costume, 1880-1920." In *Connectionalism: Ecclesiology, Mission and Identity.* Edited by Russell E. Richey, et al. Nashville: Abingdon Press, 1997, 115-34.

3247 Thorne, Roger. *Chapels, Their Architecture and Distribution: A Preliminary Bibliography.* Ottery St. Mary, England: Roger Thorn, 1994.

3248 Tucker, Karen Westerfield. "Plain and Decent: Octagonal Space and Methodist Worship." *Studia Liturgica* 24 (1994): 129-144.

3249 White, James F. "Early Methodist Liturgical Architecture." *Motive* 18 (1958): 12-13, 19-20.

3250 ———. *Protestant Worship and Church Architecture: Theological and Historical Considerations.* New York: Oxford University Press, 1964.

3251 ———. "Theology and Architecture in America: A Study of Three Leaders." In *A Miscellany of American Christianity: Essays in Honor of H. Shelton Smith*, edited by Stuart C. Henry, 362-390. Durham, NC: Duke University Press, 1963.

3252 ———, and Susan J. White. *Church Architecture: Building and Renovating for Christian Worship.* Revised edition. Akron, OH: OSL Publications, 1997.

## 14. Class Meeting

*See also Part III, Section 32: Spirituality.*

3253 Holsclaw, David F. *The Decline of Disciplined Christian Fellowship: The Methodist Class Meeting in Nineteenth-Century America.* Doctoral dissertation, University of California, Davis, 1979; Ann Arbor MI: University Microfilms International, 1979.

3254 Littell, Franklin H. "The Methodist Class Meeting as an Instrument of Christian Discipline." *World Parish* 9/1 (February 1961): 14-24.

3255 Watson, David L. *Class Leaders: Recovering a Tradition.* Nashville: Discipleship Resources, 1991.

3256 ———. *Covenant Discipleship: Christian Formation through Mutual Accountability.* Nashville: Discipleship Resources, 1991. The basic program guide, designed to be used with *Class Leaders* and *Forming Christian Disciples.*

3257 ———. *The Early Methodist Class Meeting: Its Origins and Significance.* Nashville: Discipleship Resources, 1985. The basic historical work.

3258 ———. *Forming Christian Disciples: The Role of Covenant Discipleship and Class Leaders in the Congregation.* Nashville: Discipleship Resources, 1991.

3259 Wesley, John. "The Nature, Design, and General Rules of the United Societies" (1743). In *The Works of John Wesley, Bicentennial Edition,* 9:67-75. See also "Rules and Directions to the Band Societies," 9:77-79. Both texts also in *John Wesley,* edited by Albert C. Outler, 177-81; see 4050. Cf. "The General Rules of the Methodist Church," *The Book of Discipline 1988,* 74-77 (68).

3260 ———. "A Plain Account of the People Called Methodists" (1748). In *The Works of John Wesley, Bicentennial Edition,* 9:253-280.


## 15. Ecumenism


### A. Surveys/Issues

3261 Blankenship, Paul F. *History of Negotiations for Union between Methodists and Non-Methodists in the United States.* Doctoral dissertation, Northwestern University, 1965.

3262 Deschner, John. "United Methodism's Basic Ecumenical Policy." Reprinted in *Perspectives on American Methodism,* chapter 30, 448- 459; see 3070.

3263 Holt, Ivan Lee and Elmer T. Clark. *The World Methodist Movement.* Nashville: The Upper Room, 1956.

3264 Jackson, Arland D. and Judith P. Kerr. *Ecumenical Shared Ministry and the United Methodist Church.* Moorhead, MN: CHARIS Ecumenical Center, 1995.

3265 Minus, Paul M., ed. *Methodism's Destiny in an Ecumenical Age.* New York: Abingdon Press, 1969.

3266 Outler, Albert C. *That the World May Believe: A Study of Christian Unity and What It Means for Methodists.* New York: Board of Missions, The Methodist Church, 1966.

3267 Richey, Russell E., ed. *Ecumenical and Interreligious Perspectives: Globalization in Theological Education.* Nashville: General Board of Higher Education and Ministry, UMC, 1992. Papers delivered at the Yahara Consultation of Methodist Theological Educators, March 1990.

3268 Wainwright, Geoffrey. *Methodists in Dialog.* Nashville: Kingswood Books, 1995. The basic guide to Methodist dialogues with Lutheran, Reformed, Orthodox, and Roman Catholic churches.

3269 ———. *Worship with One Accord: Where Liturgy and Ecumenism Embrace.* New York: Oxford University Press, 1997.

3270 Watley, William D. *Singing the Lord's Song in a Strange Land: The*

*African American Churches and Ecumenism*. Grand Rapids, MI: Wm. B. Eerdmans, 1993.

## B. The Ecumenical Wesley
3271 Wesley, John. "The Catholic Spirit" (1750). Sermon 39 in *The Works of John Wesley, Bicentennial Edition*, 2:81-95.
3272 ———. "Letter to a Roman Catholic" (1749). In *John Wesley*, edited by Albert C. Outler, 493-499; see 4050. For annotated edition, see *John Wesley's Letter to a Roman Catholic*, edited by Michael Hurley. Nashville: Abingdon Press, 1968.
3273 ———. "On Schism" (1786). Sermon 75 in *The Works of John Wesley, Bicentennial Edition*, 3:58-69.

## C. The Ecumenical Asbury
3274 Asbury, Francis, ed. *The Causes, Evils, and Cures of Heart and Church Divisions*. Salem, OH: Schmul Publishers, 1978. Asbury's selections from Richard Baxter and Jeremiah Burroughs. Reprint of the 1856 edition; first published in 1792.

## D. Official UMC Resolutions
The individual resolutions cited below can be found in *The Book of Resolutions of The United Methodist Church*, 1996.

3275 Act of Covenanting between other Christian Churches and The United Methodist Church, 1988.
3276 Building New Bridges in Hope, 1996.
3277 COCU Consensus: In Quest of a Church of Christian Uniting, 1988.
3278 Continuing Membership in the Consultation on Church Union, 1992.
3279 Continuing Membership in the National Council of Churches, 1992, amended & readopted 1996.
3280 Ecumenical Decade: Churches in Solidarity with Women, 1988.
3281 Ecumenical Interpretation of Doctrinal Standards, 1970, reaffirmed 1992.
3282 Guidelines for Interreligious Relationships: "Called to be Neighbors and Witnesses," 1980.
3283 Mutual Recognition of Members, 1984.
3284 Pan Methodist Unity, 1992.
3285 Proposal for the Adoption of Church in Covenant Communion, 1996.
3286 Support the Consultation on Church Union Proposal, 1996.
3287 Toward an Ecumenical Future, 1992.

## E. Anglican/Methodist International Dialogue
3288 *Sharing in the Apostolic Communion: Report of the Anglican-Methodist*

*International Commission to The World Methodist Council and the Lambeth Conference*. Lake Junaluska, NC : World Methodist Council, 1993.

### F. Anglican/Methodist Dialogue (UK)

3289    *Commitment to Mission and Unity: Report of the Informal Conversations between the Methodist Church and the Church of England.* London: Church House Publishing and Methodist Publishing House, 1996.

### G. Commission on Pan-Methodist Cooperation

3290    Consultation of Methodist Bishops. *Proceedings*, edited 1979-1991 by C. Faith Richardson; edited 1991— by Mary A. Love. 6 vols. Washington, DC, and Charlotte, NC: Secretary of the Consultation, 1979—. Reports of the first six meetings (1979, 1981, 1983, 1987, 1991, and 1995) of the bishops of the A.M.E. Church, the A.M.E. Zion Church, the Christian Methodist Episcopal Church, and the United Methodist Church to map strategy for joint action and future unity. The bishops formed the Commission on Pan-Methodist Cooperation in 1985. A joint commission to draft a plan of union was approved by all four churches in 1996.

### H. CIEMAL (Consejo de Iglesias Evangelicas Metodistas de America Latino/Council of Evangelical Methodist Churches in Latin America)

3291    In 1969, the UMC's conferences in Latin America were granted permission to become autonomous churches. At the same time, they organized themselves into this regional council together with Methodist Churches in Mexico and Cuba. The council, which celebrated its 25th anniversary in Mexico City in 1994, meets quinquennially.

### I. Consultation on Church Union (COCU)

A consultation on church union among nine churches in the USA begun in 1962. An agreed statement on covenanting rather than organic merger, adopted in 1988, was affirmed by the UMC General Conference in 1996. For official United Methodist response to the COCU plan, see appropriate resolutions in *Book of Resolutions* 1996.

3292    Consultation on Church Union. *Churches in Covenant Communion.* Princeton, NJ: COCU, 1989. Proposed plan of church unity in which member churches accept eight elements which include a common apostolic faith, recognition of members in one baptism, and mutual recognition and reconciliation of the ordained ministry. Member churches would retain their own denominational names, identity, church governments, liturgy, and patterns of ministerial training and placement.

3293 ———. *COCU Consensus: In Quest of a Church of Christ Uniting.* Princeton, NJ: COCU, 1985. Doctrinal agreement by nine parent denominations on what constitutes the core of the apostolic faith.

3294 Moede, Gerald F. *Toward Unity in Covenant Communion.* Princeton, NJ: COCU, 1988. Commentary on agreed statements and process by Methodist leader.


## J. Interreligious Dialogue

*See also Section K: Jewish/Christian Dialogue, and Section N: Muslim/Christian Dialogue.*

3295 Ariarajah, S. Wesley. "The Understanding and Practice of Dialogue: Its Nature, Purpose and Variants." In *Faith in the Midst of Faiths,* edited by S. J. Samartha. Geneva: World Council of Churches, 1977, 54-58.

3296 ———. *The Bible and People of Other Faiths.* Geneva: World Council of Churches, 1985.

3297 Berthrong, John H. *All Under Heaven: Transforming Paradigms in Confucian-Christian Dialogue.* Albany, NY: State University New York Press, 1994.

3298 Cracknell, Kenneth. *Justice, Courtesy and Love: Theologians and Missionaries Encountering World Religions, 1846-1914.* London: Epworth Press, 1995.

3299 Eck, Diana. *Encountering God: A Spiritual Journey from Bozeman to Banaras.* Boston: Beacon Press, 1993.

3300 Forward, Martin, ed. *God of All Faith: Discerning God's Presence in a Multi-Faith Society.* London: Methodist Church Home Division, 1989.

3301 ———, ed. *Ultimate Visions: Reflections on the Religions We Choose.* Oxford, England; Rockport, MA: Oneworld, 1995.

3302 Hurley, Michael J. "Salvation Today and Wesley Today." In *The Place of Wesley in the Christian Tradition,* edited by Kenneth E. Rowe. Metuchen, NJ: Scarecrow Press, 1976, 94-116.

3303 Knitter, Paul F. *No Other Name? A Critical Survey of Christian Attitudes towards the World's Religions.* London: SCM Press, 1985.

3304 Macquiban, Tim, ed. *Pure, Universal Love: Reflections on the Wesleys and Inter-Faith Dialogue.* Oxford: Westminster College, 1995.

3305 Maddox, Randy L. "Wesley as Theological Mentor: The Doctrine of Truth or Salvation through Other Religions." *Wesleyan Theological Journal* 27/1 (1992).

3306 Niles, D. T. *Buddhism and the Claims of Christ.* Richmond, VA: John Knox Press, 1967.

3307 ———. *Upon the Earth: The Mission of God and the Missionary Enterprise of the Church.* Madras: Christian Literature Society, 1963.

3308    Price, Lynne. *Interfaith Encounter and Dialogue: A Methodist Pilgrimage*. Frankfurt am Main: Peter Lang, 1991.

## K. Jewish/Christian Dialogue

3309    *Building New Bridges in Hope: The UMC on Jewish-Christian Relations.* Cincinnati: Service Center, General Board of Global Ministries, UMC, 1996. Statement adopted by the 1996 General Conference. Also in *Book of Resolutions 1996.*

3310    Klenicki, Leon and Bruce W. Robbins. *Jews and Christians: A Dialogue Service about Prayer.* Chicago: Liturgy Training Publications, 1995; New York: General Commission on Christian Unity and Interreligious Concerns, UMC, 1995.

## L. Lutheran/Methodist International Dialogue

Joint Commission between the Lutheran World Federation and the World Methodist Council, 1979-1984.

3311    "The Church: Community of Grace." Final report 1979-1984 in World Methodist Conference (15th: Nairobi, 1986) *Proceedings*, 342-360. Lake Junaluska, NC: World Methodist Council, 1987.

3312    Wainwright, Geoffrey. *Methodists in Dialog.* Nashville: Kingswood Books, 1995, 109-139.

## M. Lutheran/Methodist Dialogue (US)

*lst series, 1977- 1979*

3313    "A Lutheran-United Methodist Statement on Baptism." *Perkins Journal* 34/2 (1981): 1-56.

*2nd series, 1985-1988*

3314    *Episcopacy: A Lutheran/United Methodist Common Statement to the Church.* Cincinnati: Service Center, General Board of Global Ministries, UMC, 1987. Preliminary report.

3315    *Episcopacy: Lutheran/United Methodist Dialogue II.* Edited by Jack M. Tuell and Roger W. Fjeld. Minneapolis: Augsburg, 1991. Final report.

*3rd series, 1996-*

3316    "Realizing Unity between Lutherans and United Methodists (1996)." In *Book of Resolutions 1996*, 713-714.

## N. Muslim/Christian Dialogue

3317    "Our Muslim Neighbors, 1996" (Revision of 1992 resolution). In *Book of Resolutions 1996.*

## O. Orthodox/Methodist Dialogue

3318    Frost, Brian. *Living in Tension between East and West*. London: New World Publications, 1984.

3319    Maddox, Randy L. "John Wesley and Eastern Orthodoxy." *Asbury Theological Journal* 45/2 (Fall 1990): 29-53.

3320    *Orthodox and Methodists*. Lake Junaluska, NC: World Methodist Council, 1995. A statement by the Joint Preparatory Commission inaugurating an International Orthodox-Methodist Dialogue.

3321    Wainwright, Geoffrey. *Methodists in Dialog*. Nashville: Kingswood Books, 1995, 161-185.

## P. Reformed/Methodist International Dialogue

International Consultation between the World Alliance of Reformed Churches and the World Methodist Council.

3322    "Our Common Faith." In World Methodist Conference (15th: Nairobi, 1986) *Proceedings*, 339-342. Lake Junaluska, NC: World Methodist Council, 1987.

3323    Marshall, I. Howard. *Kept by the Power of God: A Study of Perseverance and Falling Away*. London: Epworth, 1969.

3324    Sell, Alan P. F. *The Great Debate: Calvinism, Arminianism, and Salvation*. Grand Rapids, MI: Baker Book House, 1983.

3325    "Together in God's Grace." *Reformed World* 39/8 (December 1987): 823-28.

3326    Wainwright, Geoffrey. *Geoffrey Wainwright on Wesley and Calvin: Sources for Theology, Liturgy, and Spirituality*. Melbourne: Uniting Church Press, 1987.

3327    ———. *Methodists in Dialog*. Nashville: Kingswood Books, 1995, 143-158.

## Q. Roman Catholic/Methodist International Dialogue

Joint Commission between the Roman Catholic Church and the World Methodist Council.

*1st series, 1967-1970*

3328    Denver Report. In World Methodist Conference (12th: Denver, 1971) *Proceedings*. Nashville: Abingdon Press, 1972, 39-68.

*2nd series, 1972-1975*

3329    Dublin Report. In World Methodist Conference (13th: Dublin, 1976) *Proceedings*. Lake Junaluska, NC: World Methodist Council, 1977, 254-270.

*3rd series, 1977-1981*

3330    Honolulu Report. In World Methodist Conference (14th: Honolulu,

1981) *Proceedings*. Lake Junaluska, NC: World Methodist Council, 1982, 264-277.

3331    Reports 1-3 are conveniently found in *Growth in Agreement: Reports and Agreed Statements of Ecumenical Conversations on a World Level*, edited by Harding Meyer and Lukas Vischer. Mahwah, NJ: Paulist Press, 1984, 307-387.

*4th series, 1981-1986*
3332    Nairobi Report. "Towards a Statement on the Church." In World Methodist Conference (15th: Nairobi, 1986) *Proceedings*. Lake Junaluska, NC: World Methodist Council, 1987, 360-372.

*5th series, 1986-1991*
3333    Singapore Report. *The Apostolic Tradition*. Lake Junaluska, NC: World Methodist Council, 1991. Also in World Methodist Conference (16th: Singapore, 1991) *Proceedings*. Lake Junaluska, NC: World Methodist Council, 1992, 287-310.

*6th series, 1991-1996*
3334    Rio Report. *The Word of Life: A Statement on Revelation and Faith*. Lake Junaluksa, NC : World Methodist Council, 1996. Also in World Methodist Conference (17th: Rio de Janeiro, 1996) *Proceedings*. Lake Junaluska, NC: World Methodist Council, 1997, 286- 319.

*General Studies*
3335    Butler, David. *Methodists and Papists: John Wesley and the Catholic Church in the Eighteenth Century*. London: Darton, Longman & Todd, 1995.
3336    Massa, Mark S. "The Catholic Wesley: A Revisionist Prolegomenon." *Methodist History* 22 (1983-84): 38-53.
3337    *One in Christ* 22 (1986). See articles by C. Rand, G. Tavard & G. Wainwright, and the Nairobi Report with commentary by J.-M. R. Tillard.
3338    Outler, Albert C. "An Olive Branch to the Romans, 1970s Style: United Methodist Initiative, Roman Catholic Response." *Methodist History* 13 (January 1975): 52-56. Includes full text of the 1970 General Conference "Resolution of Intent" to interpret the Articles of Religion of The UMC in the light of current ecumenical commitments, plus background, commentary and official Roman Catholic response.
3339    Tavard, George H. "For a Dialogue on Sacraments [survey of M/RC International Dialogue statements], 1967-1991." *One In Christ* 31/2 (1995): 122-145.
3340    Wainwright, Geoffrey. *Methodists in Dialog*. Nashville: Kingswood Books, 1995, 37-106.
3341    ———. *With One Accord*. Washington, DC: Pastoral Press, 1996.

### R. Roman Catholic/Methodist Dialogue (UK)

3342   *Can The Roman Catholic and Methodist Churches Be Reconciled? A Report to the Conference 1992.* Peterborough: Methodist Publishing House, 1992.

3343   *Marriages with Roman Catholics.* Peterborough: Methodist Publishing House, 1994.

3344   *Mary, Mother of the Lord, Sign of Grace, Faith, and Holiness.* Peterborough: Methodist Publishing House, 1996.


### S. Roman Catholic/Methodist Dialogue (US)

*1st series, 1966-1970*

3345   "Shared Convictions about Education, 1970."


*2nd series, 1971-1976*

3346   *Holiness and Spirituality of the Ordained Ministry.* Washington: Publication Office, United States Catholic Conference, 1976. Also in *Ecumenical Trends* 5/3 (March, 1976): 33-45.


*3rd series, 1977-1981*

3347   *Eucharistic Celebration: Converging Theology-Divergent Practice.* Cincinnati: Service Center, General Board of Global Ministries, UMC, 1981.

3348   The first three UM/RC USA reports may be found in *Building Unity: Ecumenical Dialogues with Roman Catholic Participation in the United States,* edited by Joseph A. Burgess and Jeffrey Gros, 291-322. New York: Paulist Press, 1989.


*4th series, 1986-1989*

3349   *Holy Living, Holy Dying: A United Methodist/Roman Catholic Common Statement.* Cincinnati: Service Center, General Board of Global Ministries, UMC, 1989.

3350   "Understanding Living and Dying as Faithful Christians." 1992 resolution. In *Book of Resolutions, 1996.*


*5th series, 1995-*

3351   Using Pope John Paul II's "Litany for Christian Unity" [*United Methodist Hymnal* 1989, no. 556] and his encyclical *Ut Unam Sint* [That All May Be One]. The new joint dialogue team is working on a process to help make previous discussions and understandings accessible to local parishes.


*General Study*

3352   Russalesi, Steven D. *The History of Roman Catholic-United Methodist*

*Dialogue in the United States, 1966-1989: A Theological Appraisal.* Doctoral dissertation, Catholic University of America, 1991; Ann Arbor, University Microfilms International, 1992.

## T. World Council of Churches

Three streams of ecumenical life merged in 1948 to form the WCC: Life & Work, Faith & Order, and the International Missionary Council.

3353 *Baptism, Eucharist and Ministry.* Faith & Order Paper No. 111. Geneva: World Council of Churches, 1982.

3354 *Churches Respond to BEM: Official Responses to the "Baptism, Eucharist, and Ministry" Text,* Vol. 2. Edited by Max Thurian. Geneva: World Council of Churches, 1986. See United Methodist Church (USA), 177-199; United Methodist Church (Central and Southern Europe), 200-209; Methodist Church (UK), 210-229; Methodist Church in Ireland, 230-235; Methodist Church of South Africa, 236-244; and Waldensian and Methodist Churches in Italy, 245-254.

3355 Deschner, John. "The Changing Shape of the Church Unity Question." In *Faith and Order 1985-1989: The Commission Meeting at Budapest, 1989,* edited by Thomas F. Best. Faith & Order Paper No. 148. Geneva: World Council of Churches, 1990, 44-54.

3356 ———. "The Unity of the Church and the Renewal of the Human Community." In *Towards Visible Unity: Commission on Faith and Order, 1982,* edited by Michael Kinnamon. Faith & Order Paper No. 113. Geneva: World Council of Churches, 1982, 184-197.

3357 Wainwright, Geoffrey. *Methodists in Dialog.* Nashville: Kingswood Books, 1995, 189-228.

## U. World Federation of Methodist and United Church Women

A global fellowship of women in churches either affiliated with the World Methodist Council or in a united church of which former Methodists are a part. Begun in 1939, the federation holds world assemblies once every five years.

3358 Keller, Rosemary, ed. *Methodist Women: A World Sisterhood: A History of the World Federation of Methodist Women, 1923-1986.* [New York]: World Federation of Methodist Women, 1986.

3359 *Handbook of the World Federation of Methodist and United Church Women, 1996-2001.* Cincinnati : Service Center, General Board of Global Ministries, 1997. Published quinquennially.

## V. World Methodist Council

An association of the world family of Methodist churches. World conferences, held on a regular basis since 1881, were called Ecumenical Methodist Conferences from 1881 to 1947.

3360 *Saved by Grace: A Statement of World Methodist Belief and Practice.* Lake Junaluska, NC: World Methodist Council, 1996.

3361 "World Methodist Social Affirmation" (adopted by the 1986 conference). In *United Methodist Hymnal* 1989, No. 886.

3362 *World Methodist Council Handbook of Information, 1997-2002.* Lake Junaluska, NC: World Methodist Council, 1997. Published quinquennially.

3363 Tuttle, Lee F. *A Quinquennium in Review.* Lake Junaluska, NC: World Methodist Council, 1966-1976. 3 vols, 1961-66, 1966-71, 1971-76.


## 16. Ethnicity
*See also separate sections on African, Asian,*
*Hispanic, and Native American Methodists.*


3364 Andersen, Arlo W. *The Salt of the Earth: A History of Norwegian-Danish Methodism in America.* Nashville: Parthenon Press, 1962.

3365 Douglass, Paul F. *The Story of German Methodism: Biography of an Immigrant Soul.* New York: Methodist Book Concern, 1939.

3366 González, Justo L. *Out of Every Tribe and Nation: Christian Theology at the Ethnic Roundtable.* Nashville: Abingdon Press, 1992.

3367 Mangano, Antonio. *Religious Work among Italians in America: A Survey for the Home Missions Council.* Philadelphia: Board of Home Missions and Church Extension of the Methodist Episcopal Church, 1917.

3368 Sano, Roy I. *From Every Nation Without Number: Racial and Ethnic Diversity in United Methodism.* Nashville: Abingdon Press, 1982.

3369 Whyman, Henry C. *The Hedstroms's and the Bethelship Saga.* Carbondale, IL: Southern Illinois University Press, 1992.

3370 ———. *The History of Ethnic Ministries in the New York Conference, The United Methodist Church.* New York: New York Conference Bicentennial Committee, 1984.

3371 Wimberly, Anne S. *Language of Hospitality: Intercultural Relations in the Household of God.* Nashville: Cokesbury Press, 1991. An official resource prepared by the General Board of Discipleship through the Division of Church School Publications.

3372 *Words That Hurt and Words That Heal: Language about God and People.* New edition. Nashville: Graded Press, 1991. Leader's guide plus full text of document prepared in 1988 by the United Methodist Task Force on Language Guidelines.

## 17. Evangelical and United Brethren Traditions

3373    Albright, Raymond W. *A History of The Evangelical Church*. Harrisburg, PA: Evangelical Press, 1942. Reprinted many times.

3374    Behney, J. Bruce and Paul H. Eller. *The History of the Evangelical United Brethren Church*. Nashville: Abingdon Press, 1979.

3375    Breyfogel, Sylvanus C. *Landmarks of the Evangelical Association, Containing All of the Official Records of the Annual and the General Conferences from the Days of Jacob Albright to the Year 1840*. Reading, PA: Eagle Book Print, 1888.

3376    Drury, Augustus W. *History of the Church of the United Brethren in Christ*. Revised edition. Dayton, OH: Otterbein Press, 1931. First published in 1924.

3377    ————, ed. *Minutes of the Annual and General Conferences of the Church of the United Brethren in Christ, 1800-1818*. Nashville: Parthenon Press, 1996. Reprint of 1897 edition.

3378    Longenecker, Stephen. *Piety and Tolerance: Pennsylvania German Religion, 1700-1850*. Metuchen, NJ : Scarecrow Press, 1994.

3379    Miller, George. *Practical Christianity; or, Short and Plain Doctrines Setting Forth True Godliness*. Nashville: Parthenon Press, 1996. Reprint of the Cleveland: Evangelical Association Publishing House, 1871, English translation of Miller's *Das thatige Christenthum; oder, Kurze und deutliche Lehren zur Beförderung wahrer Gottseligkeit*. 2. und verb. Aufl. Neu-Berlin, PA: J.C.Reissner, fur die Evangelische Gemeinschaft, 1844. First published in Reading, PA, by G. Jungman, 1814.

3380    O'Malley, J. Steven. *Early German American Evangelicalism: Pietist Sources on Discipleship and Sanctification*. Lanham, MD: Scarecrow Press, 1995.

## 18. Evangelical Methodists
*See also Section 23: Holiness Movement.*

3381    Dayton, Donald W. *Discovering an Evangelical Heritage*. Peabody, MA: Hendrickson Publishers, 1988. Reprint of the 1976 edition.

3382    Heidinger, James. "The United Methodist Church." In *Evangelical Renewal in the Mainline Churches*, edited by Ronald H. Nash. Westchester, IL: Crossway Books, 1987, 15-39.

3383    Keysor, Charles W. "Methodism's Silent Minority: A Voice for Orthodoxy." *Christian Advocate* 10 (July 14, 1966): 9-10. Founding article for the Good News movement.

3384 ———. "The Story of Good News." *Good News* 14 (March-April 1981). Special issue.

3385 McCutcheon, William J. and William Neill. "United Methodist Evangelicals in Two Generations: The 1920s and the 1930s." *Explor* 2/2 (Fall 1976): 59-72.

3386 Nash, Ronald H. *Evangelical Renewal in the Mainline Churches.* Westchester, IL: Crossway Books, 1987. See especially chapter on The UMC by James D. Heidinger.

3387 Spann, Howard Glen. *Evangelicalism in Modern American Methodism: Theological Conservatives in the "Great Deep" of the Church, 1900-1980.* Doctoral dissertation, Johns Hopkins University, 1995.

3388 Sweet, Leonard I., ed. *The Evangelical Tradition in America.* Macon, GA: Mercer University Press, 1984.


## 19. Evangelism


3389 Abraham, William J. *The Art of Evangelism.* Sheffield, England: Cliff College Publishing, 1993.

3390 Arias, Mortimer. *Announcing the Reign of God: Evangelization and the Subversive Message of Jesus.* Philadelphia: Fortress Press, 1984.

3391 ——— and Alan Johnson. *The Great Commission: Biblical Models for Evangelism.* Nashville: Abingdon Press, 1992.

3392 Dunnam, Maxie D. *Going on to Salvation: A Study in the Wesleyan Tradition.* Nashville: Discipleship Resources, 1990.

3393 Harding, Joe A. and Ralph W. Mohney. *Vision 2000: Planning for Ministry into the Next Century.* Nashville: Discipleship Resources, 1991.

3394 Hunter, George G., III. *To Spread the Power: Church Growth in the Wesleyan Spirit.* Nashville: Abingdon Press, 1987.

3395 Logan, James C., ed. *Christ for the World: United Methodist Bishops Speak on Evangelism.* Nashville: Kingswood Books, 1996.

3396 ———, ed. *Theology and Evangelism in the Wesleyan Heritage.* Nashville: Kingswood Books, 1994.

3397 Morris, George E. and H. Eddie Fox, *Faith-Sharing: Dynamic Christian Witnessing by Invitation.* Revised and expanded edition. Nashville: Discipleship Resources, 1996.

3398 Outler, Albert C. *Evangelism and Theology in the Wesleyan Spirit.* Nashville: Discipleship Resources, 1996. Reissue of two 1971 works by Outler combined into one publication.

3399 Swanson, Roger K. and Shirley F. Clement. *The Faith-Sharing Con-

*gregation: Developing Strategies for the Congregation as Evangelist.* Nashville: Discipleship Resources, 1996.

3400 Tuttle, Robert G., Jr. *On Giant Shoulders: The History, Role and Influence of the Evangelist in the Movement Called Methodism.* Nashville: Discipleship Resources, 1984.

3401 United Methodist Church, Council of Bishops. *Vital Congregations/Faithful Disciples: Vision for the Church.* Nashville: Graded Press, 1990. Pastoral Letter, foundation document, leader's guide, and video.

## 20. Healing and Health Care

3402 Official UMC Resolutions: "Health and Wholeness," 1984; "Universal Access to Health Care," 1992. *Book of Resolutions 1996*, 274-78, 424-27.

3403 Crouch, Timothy J., ed. and comp. *A United Methodist Rite for Anointing.* Cleveland: Order of St. Luke Publications, 1986.

3404 Crummey, David C. *Factors in the Rise of Methodist Hospitals and Homes.* Doctoral dissertation, University of Chicago, 1963.

3405 Day, Albert E. *Letters on the Healing Ministry*, with study guide by James K. Wagner. Nashville: The Upper Room, 1986. Reprint of 1946 edition.

3406 *Health For All Manual: A Congregational Health Ministries Resource.* Cincinnati: Health & Welfare Ministries, General Board of Global Ministries, UMC, 1997.

3407 Hill, A. Wesley. *John Wesley among the Physicians: A Study of 18th-Century Medicine.* London: Epworth Press, 1958.

3408 Holifield, E. Brooks. *Health and Medicine in the Methodist Tradition.* New York: Crossroads/Continuum, 1986.

3409 Stanger, Frank Bateman. *God's Healing Community.* Wilmore, KY: Francis Asbury Publishing Company, 1985. Reprint of 1978 Abingdon edition.

3410 Wagner, James K. *An Adventure in Healing and Wholeness: The Healing Ministry in the Church Today.* Nashville: Upper Room Books, 1993.

3411 ———. *Blessed to Be a Blessing: How to Have an Intentional Healing Ministry in Your Church.* Nashville: The Upper Room, 1980.

3412 Wesley, John. "On Visiting the Sick" (1786). Sermon 98 in *The Works of John Wesley, Bicentennial Edition*, 3:384-397.

3413 ———. *Primitive Remedies.* Santa Barbara, CA: Woodbridge Press Publishing Co., 1973. Reprint of 1755 edition.

3414 ———. *Wesley's Primitive Physick.* Library of Methodist Classics. Nashville: United Methodist Publishing House, 1992. Facsimile reprint of the first printing by the Methodists in America, 1791.

## 21. Higher Education
*For works on Theological Education, see Part IV, Section 6.*

3415    Bowser, Beth A. *Living the Vision: The University Senate of the Methodist Episcopal Church, The Methodist Church, and The United Methodist Church, 1892-1991.* Nashville: Board of Higher Education and Ministry, UMC, 1992.

3416    Cole, Charles E., ed. *Something More Than Human: Biographies of Leaders in American Methodist Higher Education.* Nashville: General Board of Higher Education and Ministry, UMC, 1986.

3417    Cuninggim, Merrimon. *Uneasy Partners: The College and the Church.* Nashville: Abingdon Press, 1994.

3418    Dent, Frank Lloyd. *"Motive" Magazine: Advocating the Arts and Empowering the Imagination in the Life of the Church.* Doctoral dissertation, Columbia University, 1989.

3419    Duvall, Sylvanus M. *The Methodist Episcopal Church and Education up to 1869.* New York: Bureau of Publications, Teacher's College, Columbia University, 1928.

3420    Fedje, Raymond Norman. *The Wesley Foundation: A Selective History.* Doctoral dissertation, Boston University, 1964.

3421    Johnson, Terrell E. *A History of Methodist Education and its Influence on American Public Education.* Doctoral dissertation, Southern Illinois University at Carbondale, 1989.

3422    Marsden, Gerorge M. and Bradley J. Longfield, eds. *The Secularization of the Academy.* New York: Oxford University Press, 1992.

3423    Marsden, George M. *The Soul of the American University: From Protestant Establishment to Established Nonbelief.* New York: Oxford University Press, 1994.

3424    Morrison, Theodore. *Chautauqua: A Center for Education, Religion and the Arts in America.* Chicago: University of Chicago Press, 1974.

3425    Sloan, Douglas. *Faith and Knowledge: Mainline Protestantism and American Higher Education.* Louisville, KY: Westminster/John Knox, 1994.

## 22. Hispanic American Methodists
*See also Part III, Section 5: Central and South America.*

3426    Garza, Minerva N. "The Influence of Methodism on Hispanic Women through Women's Societies." *Methodist History* 34/2 (January 1996): 78-89.

3427    González, Justo L., ed. *Each in Our Own Tongue: A History of Hispanic*

*United Methodism.* Nashville: Abingdon Press, 1991. Also available in Spanish: *En Nuestra Propria Lengua.* The basic work.

3428 ——, ed. *Voces: Voices from the Hispanic Church.* Nashville: Abingdon Press, 1992.

3429 Gray, C. Jarrett, Jr., comp. *The Racial and Ethnic Presence in American Methodism: A Bibliography.* Madison, NJ: General Commission on Archives and History, UMC, 1991.

3430 Harwood, Thomas. *History of the New Mexico, Spanish and English Missions of the Methodist Episcopal Church from 1850 to 1910.* 2 vols. Albuquerque, NM: El Abogado Press, 1908-1910.

3131 *The Hispanic Vision for Century III.* San Antonio, TX: MARCHA, the National Hispanic United Methodist Caucus, 1985.

3132 Náñez, Alfredo. *History of the Rio Grande Conference of The United Methodist Church.* Dallas: Bridwell Library, Southern Methodist University, 1981. Also available in Spanish.

3133 Nanez, Clotilde. "Hispanic Clergy Wives: Their Contribution to United Methodism in the Southwest." In *Women in New Worlds.* Edited by Hilah Thomas, et al. Nashville: Abingdon Press, 1981, I:161-177.

3434 National Plan for Hispanic Ministries. Text of plan in *Book of Resolutions 1996.* Text and manuals in English and Spanish available from Discipleship Resources.

3435 Recinos, Harold J. *Hear the Cry!: A Latino Pastor Challenges the Church.* Louisville, KY: Westminster/John Knox Press, 1989.


## 23. Holiness Movement


Includes historical works on the Church of the Nazarene, Free Methodist, and Wesleyan Methodist traditions in the United States. *See also Part III, Section 9: Camp Meetings, Section 18: Evangelical Methodists, and Part IV, Section 5: History of Doctrine.*

3436 Brasher, J. Lawrence. *The Sanctified South: John Lakin Brasher and the Holiness Movement.* Urbana: University of Illinois Press, 1994.

3437 Caldwell, Wayne E., ed. *Reformers and Revivalists.* Indianapolis: Wesley Press, 1992. (Wesleyan History series, Vol. 3.)

3438 Dayton, Donald W. *Discovering an Evangelical Heritage.* Peabody, MA: Hendrickson Publishers, 1988. Reprint of the 1976 edition.

3439 ——. "From 'Christian Perfection' to the 'Baptism of the Holy Ghost.'" Reprinted in *Perspectives on American Methodism,* chapter 18, 289-297; see 3070.

3440   ———. *The Theological Roots of Pentecostalism*. Metuchen, NJ: Scarecrow Press, 1987.

3441   Dieter, Melvin E. *The Holiness Revival of the Nineteenth Century*. Revised
edition. Lanham, MD: Scarecrow Press, 1996. The basic work.

3442   Haines, Lee M. and Paul William Thomas. *An Outline History of the
Wesleyan Church*. 3d revised edition. Marion, IN: Wesley Press, 1985.

3443   Jones, Charles E. *A Guide to the Study of the Holiness Movement*.
Metuchen, NJ: Scarecrow Press, 1974.

3444   ———. *Perfectionist Persuasion: The Holiness Movement and American
Methodism, 1867-1936*. Metuchen, NJ: Scarecrow Press, 1974.

3445   Kostlevy, William. *Holiness Manuscripts: A Guide to Sources Document-
ing the Wesleyan Holiness Movement in the United States and Canada*.
Metuchen, NJ: Scarecrow Press, 1994.

3446   McKenna, David L. *A Future with a History: The Wesleyan Witness
of the Free Methodist Church*. Indianapolis: Light and Life Press,
1995.

3447   McLeister, Ira Ford. *Conscience and Commitment: The History of the
Wesleyan Methodist Church of America*. 4th revised edition. Wesleyan
History series, Vol. 1. Marion, IN: Wesley Press, 1976.

3448   Marston, Leslie Ray. *From Age to Age a Living Witness: A Historical
Interpretation of Free Methodism's First Hundred Years*. Winona Lake,
IN: Light and Life Press, 1960.

3449   Miller, William C. *Holiness Works: A Bibliography*. Revised edition.
Kansas City, MO: Beacon Hill Press, 1986.

3450   Reinhard, James Arnold. *Personal and Sociological Factors in the Formation of the Free Methodist Church*. Doctoral dissertation, University of
Iowa, 1971.

3451   Smith, Timothy L. *Called unto Holiness: The Story of the Nazarenes, the
Formative Years*. Kansas City: Nazarene Publishing House, 1962. 2
vols. Vol. 2 by W. T. Purkiser.

3452   ———. "The Holiness Crusade." In *History of American Methodism*,
edited by Emory S. Bucke, 2:608-627; see 3056.

3453   ———. *Revivalism and Social Reform: American Protestantism on the Eve
of the Civil War*. Baltimore, MD: Johns Hopkins University Press,
1980. Reprint of 1957 edition.

3454   Thomas, Paul W. *The Days of our Pilgrimage: The History of the Pilgrim
Holiness Church*. Wesleyan History series, Vol. 2. Marion, IN: Wesley
Press, 1976.

3455   Walls, Francine E. *The Free Methodist Church: A Bibliography*. Winona
Lake, IN: Free Methodist Historical Center, 1977.

## 24. Human Sexuality

3456    Abelove, Henry. *The Evangelist of Desire: John Wesley and the Methodists.* Stanford, CA: Stanford University Press, 1990. See chapter 5, "Sexuality."

3457    Babuscio, Jack. *We Speak for Ourselves: The Experiences of Gay Men and Lesbians.* Nashville: Abingdon Press, 1991.

3458    Blair, Ralph. *Wesleyan Praxis and Homosexual Practice.* New York: HCCC, Inc., 1983.

3459    Brash, Alan A. *Facing Our Differences: The Churches and Their Gay and Lesbian Neighbors.* New York: World Council of Churches, 1995.

3460    Carey, John J., ed. *The Sexuality Debate in North American Churches 1988-1995: Controversies, Unresolved Issues, Future Prospects.* Lewiston, NY: Edwin Mellen Press, 1995.

3461    *The Church Studies Homosexuality: A Study Guide for United Methodist Groups Using the Report of the Committee to Study Homosexuality.* Nashville: Cokesbury, 1994. Study book with full text of the Committee to Study Homosexuality to the General Conference of 1992, and commentary plus leader's guide by Dorothy L. Williams. 2 vols.

3462    Furnish, Victor P., et al. *Homosexuality in Search of a Christian Understanding: Biblical, Theological-Ethical, and Pastoral Care Perspectives.* Nashville: Discipleship Resources, 1981.

3463    Geis, Sally B. and Donald E. Messer, eds. *Caught in the Crossfire: Helping Christians Debate Homosexuality.* Nashville : Abingdon Press, 1994.

3464    Hartman, Keith. *Congregations in Conflict: The Battle over Homosexuality in Nine Churches.* New Brunswick, NJ: Rutgers University Press, 1996.

3465    Hilton, Bruce. *Can Homophobia Be Cured? Wrestling with Questions That Challenge the Church.* Nashville: Abingdon Press, 1992.

3466    Keysor, Charles W., ed. *What You Should Know about Homosexuality.* Grand Rapids, MI: Zondervan Publishing House, 1979.

3467    Koehler, George E. *Guide to the Study Document on Human Sexuality.* Nashville: Discipleship Resources, 1983. Includes the full text of the 1980 General Conference "Study Document on Human Sexuality."

3468    Methodist Church (Great Britain) Commission on Human Sexuality. *Report of the Commission on Human Sexuality.* Peterborough: Methodist Publishing House, 1990.

3469    ———. *Human Sexuality: A Study Guide to the Report Presented to the Methodist Conference 1990.* London: Methodist Publishing House, 1991.

3470    Mickey, Paul A. *Of Sacred Worth.* Nashville: Abingdon Press, 1991.

3471    Osterman, Mary Jo. *Claiming the Promise.* Chicago: Reconciling Congregation Program, 1997. Bible study resource on homosexuality.

3472 "Our History: Affirmation Time-Line." *Affirmation Newsletter* 1 (Summer 1989): 3-4.

3473 *Still on the Journey: A Handbook for Reconciling Congregations.* Chicago: Reconciling Congregations Program, 1994.

3474 *Thinking It Through: United Methodists Look at the Church and Homosexuality.* Revised edition. Staten Island, NY: Methodist Federation for Social Action, 1990. Comprehensive study packet.

3475 "Timeline: 25 Years of the Lesbian/Gay Christian Movement." *Open Hands* 5/3 (Winter 1990): 10-13.

## 25. Hymnology

3476 Berger, Teresa. *Theology in Hymns? A Study of the Relationship of Doxology and Theology according to the "Collection of Hymns for the Use of the People Called Methodists" (1780).* Nashville: Kingswood Books, 1995.

3477 *Companion to Hymns & Psalms.* Edited by Richard Watson and Kenneth Trickett. Peterborough, UK: Methodist Publishing House, 1988.

3478 Cone, James H. *The Spirituals and the Blues: An Interpretation.* Philadelphia: Winston, 1972.

3479 Deschner, Roger. "Methodist Church, Music of the." In *The New Grove Dictionary of American Music.* New York: Macmillan, 1986, III: 217-220

3480 Kimbrough, S. T., Jr. *A Heart to Praise My God: Wesley Hymns Today.* Nashville: Abingdon Press, 1996.

3481 ———. *Lost in Wonder: Charles Wesley, the Meaning of His Hymns Today.* Nashville: The Upper Room, 1987.

3482 Lawson, John. *The Wesley Hymns as a Guide to Scriptural Teaching.* Grand Rapids, MI: Zondervan Publishing House, 1988.

3483 Lorenz, Ellen Jane. *Glory Hallelujah: The Story of the Camp Meeting Spiritual.* Nashville: Abingdon Press, 1980.

3484 Rattenbury, John E. *The Evangelical Doctrines of Charles Wesley's Hymns.* London: Epworth Press, 1941.

3485 ———. *The Eucharistic Hymns of John and Charles Wesley.* London: Epworth Press, 1948. Revised edition. Cleveland, OH: Order of St. Luke Publications, 1990.

3486 Rogal, Samuel J., comp. *Guide to the Hymns and Tunes of American Methodism.* New York: Greenwood Press, 1986. A reference guide to the 3,901 hymns and tunes included in six major Methodist hymnals, 1878 to 1964.

3487 Sanchez, Diana, ed. *The Hymns of The United Methodist Hymnal.* Nashville: Abingdon Press, 1989.

3488 Schilling, S. Paul. *The Faith We Sing.* Philadelphia: Westminster Press, 1983.

3489 Sizer, Sandra. *Gospel Hymns and Social Religion: The Rhetoric of Nineteenth-Century Revivalism.* Philadelphia: Temple University Press, 1978.

3490 Spencer, Jon Michael. *Protest and Praise: Sacred Music of Black Religion.* Minneapolis: Fortress Press, 1990.

3491 ———. *Black Hymnology: A Hymnological History of the African-American Church.* Knoxville, TN: University of Tennessee Press, 1992.

3492 Warren, James I. *O for a Thousand Tongues to Sing: The History, Nature and Influence of Music in the Methodist Tradition.* Grand Rapids, MI: Francis Asbury Press of Zondervan Publishing House, 1988.

3493 Yoder, Don. *Pennsylvania Spirituals.* Lancaster, PA: Pennsylvania Folklore Society, 1961. A basic work on early EUB folk hymnody.

3494 Young, Carlton R. *Companion to the 1989 Hymnal.* Nashville: Abingdon Press, 1992. The basic work.

3495 ———. *Music of the Heart: John & Charles Wesley on Music and Musicians: An Anthology.* Carol Stream, IL: Hope Publishing Co., 1995

## 26. Missions

*See also Section 15: Ecumenism, Subsection J, Interreligious Dialogue, and Section 33: Women.*

3496 Barclay, Wade C. *History of Methodist Missions.* 4 vols. New York: Board of Missions, The Methodist Church, 1949-1973.

3497 Behney, J. Bruce, and Paul H. Eller. *The History of the Evangelical United Brethren Church.* Nashville: Abingdon Press, 1979. Helpful index.

3498 Davey, Cyril. *Changing Places: Methodist Mission Then and Now.* Basingstoke, UK: Marshall Morgan and Scott, 1988.

3499 Hill, Patricia R. *The World Their Household: The American Woman's Foreign Mission Movement and Cultural Transformation, 1870-1920.* Ann Arbor, MI: University of Michigan Press, 1985.

3500 Hunter, Jane. *The Gospel of Gentility: American Women Missionaries in Turn-of-the-Century-China.* New Haven: Yale University Press, 1984.

3501 Hutchison, William R. *Errand to the World: American Protestant Thought and Foreign Missions.* Chicago: University of Chicago Press, 1987.

3502 Maclin, H. T. *The Faith That Compels Us: Reflections on the Mission*

*Society for United Methodists, The First Decade 1984-1994*. Norcross, GA: Mission Society for United Methodists, 1997.

3503 O'Malley, J. Steven. "The Vision of German-American Evangelicalism: The Central Role of Missions in the Evangelical United Brethren Tradition." *Methodist History* 34 (April 1996): 148-172.

3504 *Partnership in God's Mission: Theology of Mission Statement*. New York: General Board of Global Ministries, 1986.

3505 Robert, Dana L., *American Women in Mission: A Social History of Their Thought and Practice*. Macon, GA: Mercer University Press, 1996.

3506 Vickers, John A. "One-Man Band: Thomas Coke and the Origins of Methodist Missions, 1760-1814." *Methodist History* 34 (1995-96): 135-147.

## 27. Native American Methodists

3507 Bowden, Henry W. *American Indians and Christian Missions: Studies in Cultural Conflict*. Chicago: University of Chicago Press, 1981.

3508 Copway, George. *Indian Life and Indian History*. New York: AMS Press, 1976. Reprint of the 1860 edition.

3509 *Eagle Flights: Native Americans and the Christian Faith*. Nashville: Graded Press, 1996. Students' book plus leader's guide.

3510 Finley, James B. *Life among the Indians; or, Personal Reminiscences and Historical Incidents Illustrative of Indian Life and Character*. Edited by D. W. Clark. New York: Ayer Co., 1976. Reprint of 1857 edition.

3511 Forbes, Bruce D. " 'And Obey God, etc.': Methodism and American Indians." *Methodist History* 23/1 (October 1984): 3-24. Reprinted in *Perspectives on American Methodism*, chapter 13, 209-227; see 3070.

3512 ———. "Methodist Mission among the Dakotas: A Case Study of Difficulties." In *Rethinking Methodist History*, edited by Russell E. Richey and Kenneth E. Rowe, 48-58; see 3070.

3513 Gray, C. Jarrett, Jr., comp. *The Racial and Ethnic Presence in American Methodism: A Bibliography*. Madison, NJ: General Commission on Archives and History, UMC, 1991.

3514 McLoughlin, William G. *Cherokees and Missionaries, 1789-1839*. New Haven: Yale University Press, 1984.

3515 ———. "Cherokees and Christianity, 1794-1870." *Essays on Acculturation and Cultural Persistence*. Athens, GA: University of Georgia Press, 1994.

3516 Milner, Clyde A. and Floyd A. O'Neill, eds. *Churchmen and the Western Indians*. Norman, OK: University of Oklahoma Press, 1985. See especially article by Bruce Forbes on Methodist missions.

3517 Native American International Caucus. *The Sacred Circle of Life: A Native American Vision*. Norwalk, CA: Native American International Caucus, 1988.

3518 Noley, Homer, ed. *First White Frost: Native Americans and United Methodism*. Nashville: Abingdon Press, 1991. The basic work.

3519 Norwood, Frederick A. "The Invisible American: Methodism and the Indian." *Methodist History* 8/2 (January 1970): 3-24.

3520 Tinker, George. *Missionary Conquest: The Gospel and Native American Genocide*. Minneapolis: Fortress Press, 1993.

3521 "The United Methodist Church and America's Native People, 1980." In *Book of Resolutions 1996*, 178-181.

## 28. Peace

3522 *In Defense of Creation: The Nuclear Crisis and a Just Peace*. Nashville: Graded Press, 1986. The Bishops' Pastoral Letter, the foundation document, and guide for study and action.

3523 Mills, W. Douglas. "The Response of the Methodist Church to War and Nuclear Weapons 1945-1990." *Quarterly Review* 17/3 (Fall 1997): 257-274.

3524 Will, Herman. *A Will for Peace: Peace Action in the United Methodist Church, A History*. Washington: General Board of Church and Society, UMC, 1984.

3525 Wilson, Robert W. *Biases and Blindspots: Methodism and Foreign Policy from World War II*. Wilmore, KY: Bristol Books, 1988.

**Pentecostal Methodists, see Section 11:
Charismatic/Pentecostal Movement.**

## 29. Preaching
*See also Part IV, Sections 11-12: The Ministry of Elders,
Bishops, and Superintendents.*

3526 Abbey, Merrill R. *The Epic of United Methodist Preaching: A Profile in American Social History*. Lanham, MD: University Press of America, 1984.

3527 Crawford, Evans E. and Thomas H. Troeger. *The Hum: Call and Response in African American Preaching*. Nashville: Abingdon Press, 1996.

3528    Heitzenrater, Richard P. "Spirit and Life: John Wesley's Preaching." In *Mirror and Memory: Reflections on Early Methodism*, 162-173; see 3027.

3529    ———. "Wesley as Preacher." In his *The Elusive Mr. Wesley*, 2:83-89.

3530    ———. "Early Sermons of John and Charles Wesley." In *Mirror and Memory: Reflections on Early Methodism*, 150-161.

3531    Lawrence, William B. *Sundays in New York: Pulpit Theology at the Crest of the Protestant Mainstream, 1930-1955*. Lanham, MD: Scarecrow Press, 1996.

3532    Lee, Jung Young. *Korean Preaching: An Interpretation*. Nashville: Abingdon Press, 1997.

3533    Outler, Albert C. *John Wesley's Sermons: An Introduction*. Nashville: Abingdon Press, 1991. Originally published in *The Works of John Wesley, Bicentennial Edition*, 1:1-100.

3534    Spencer, Jon Michael. *Sacred Symphony: The Chanted Sermon of the Black Preacher*. New York: Greenwood Press, 1988.

3535    Wesley, John. "Address to the Clergy" (1756). In *The Works of John Wesley*, edited by Thomas Jackson, 10:480-500.

3536    ———. "Of Preaching Christ" (1751). In *The Works of John Wesley*, edited by Thomas Jackson, 11:486-492.

3537    ———. "Thoughts Concerning Gospel Ministers" (1784). In *The Works of John Wesley*, edited by Thomas Jackson, 7:455-456.

## 30. Publishing and Communications

3538    Cumbers, Frank H. *The Book Room: The Story of the Methodist Publishing House and Epworth Press*. London: Epworth Press, 1956.

3539    Ness, John H., Jr. *One Hundred Fifty Years: A History of Publishing in the Evangelical United Brethren Church*. Nashville: Abingdon Press, 1966.

3540    Pilkington, James P. *The Methodist Publishing House: A History*, Vol. 1. Nashville: Abingdon Press, 1968. The basic history to 1870. Continued by Walter N. Vernon, *The History of The United Methodist Publishing House*, Vol. 2. Nashville: Abingdon Press, 1988. The basic history from 1870 to 1968.

3541    Maynard, Edwin H. *Keeping Up with a Revolution: The Story of United Methodist Communications, 1940-1990*. Nashville: United Methodist Communications, 1990.

3542    Sweet, Leonard I., ed. *Communication and Change in American Religious History*. Grand Rapids, MI: Wm. B. Eerdmans, 1993.

## 31. Social Thought and Action

*See also Part IV, Section 16: Theological Ethics.*

### A. Official Statements

3543   "Social Principles." *Book of Discipline 1996*, Part III, par. 64-120. Use with next item.

3544   *The Book of Resolutions of the United Methodist Church*, 1996. Nashville: United Methodist Publishing House, 1996. Includes all valid resolutions since 1968, plus topical index.

3545   Methodist Church (Great Britain). *Statements on Social Responsibility, 1946-1995*. Peterborough: Methodist Publishing House, 1996.

### B. Commentary and History

3546   Black, Kathy. *A Healing Homiletic: Preaching and Disabilities*. Nashville: Abingdon Press, 1996.

3547   Brewer, Earl D. C. and Scott L. Thumma. *World Methodism and World Issues*. Atlanta: Center for Religious Research, Candler School of Theology, Emory University, 1990.

3548   Cameron, Richard M. *Methodism and Society in Historical Perspective*. Nashville: Abingdon Press, 1961.

3549   Eli, R. George. *Social Holiness: John Wesley's Thinking on Christian Commmunity and its Relationship to the Social Order*. New York: Peter Lang, 1993.

3550   Gorrell, Donald K. *The Age of Social Responsibility: The Social Gospel in the Progressive Era, 1900-1920*. Macon, GA: Mercer University Press, 1988.

3551   ———. "The Social Creed and Methodism through Eighty Years." *Methodist History* 26/4 (July 1988): 213-228. Reprinted in *Perspectives on American Methodism*, chapter 26, 386-399; see 3070.

3552   Harkness, Georgia. *The Methodist Church in Social Thought and Action*. Nashville: Abingdon Press, 1972.

3553   Henning, Robert James. *Methodist Response to Labor Unrest in Late Nineteenth Century America: A Cultural Theory*. Doctoral dissertation, Michigan State University, 1994.

3554   Jennings, Theodore W. *Good News to the Poor: John Wesley's Evangelical Economics*. Nashville: Abingdon Press, 1990.

3555   *Journey Toward Justice: Consultation Celebrating the 80th Anniversary of the Social Creed*. Staten Island NY : Methodist Federation for Social Action, 1988.

3556   Kehrburg, Norma. *Love in Action: UMCOR, 50 Years of Service*. Nashville: Abingdon Press, 1989.

3557   Knepper, Jeanne Gayle. *Thy Kingdom Come: The Methodist Federation for Social Service and Human Rights, 1907-1948.* Staten Island, New York : Methodist Federation for Social Action, 1996.

3558    Letzig, Betty J. *Expressions of Faith.* Cincinnati: Service Center, General Board of Global Ministries, UMC, 1990. A study of the social welfare institutions of the National Division of GBGM.

3559    Long, Stephen D. *Living the Discipline: United Methodist Theological Reflection on War, Civilization and Holiness.* Grand Rapids, MI: Eerdmans, 1992.

3560    McClain, George D. *Claiming All Things for God: Prayer, Discernment, and Ritual for Social Change.* Nashville: Abingdon Press, 1998

3561    ———. "Pioneering Social Gospel Radicalism: An Overview of the History of the Methodist Federation for Social Action." Reprinted in *Perspectives on American Methodism,* chapter 25, 371-385; see 3070.

3562    Meeks, M. Douglas, ed. *The Portion of the Poor: Good News to the Poor in the Wesleyan Tradition.* Nashville: Kingswood Books, 1992.

3563    *Methodist Federation for Social Service/Action.* Special issue of *Radical Religion* 5 (1980). Copies available from MFSA office.

3564    Muelder, Walter G. *Methodism and Society in the Twentieth Century.* Nashville: Abingdon Press, 1961.

3565    Schmidt, Jean Miller. "Reexamining the Public/Private Split: Reforming the Continent and Spreading Scriptural Holiness." Reprinted in *Perspectives on American Methodism,* chapter 14, 228-247; see 3070.

3566    ———. *Souls or the Social Order: The Two-Party System in American Protestantism.* New York: Carlson, 1991.

3567    Seifert, Harvey. *What on Earth: Making Personal Decisions on Controversial Issues.* Nashville: Discipleship Resources for Church and Society, 1986.

3568    Stevens, Thelma. *Legacy for the Future: History of Christian Social Relations in the Woman's Division of Christian Service, 1940-1968.* Cincinnati: General Board of Global Ministries, UMC, 1978.

3569    Walsh, John D. "John Wesley and the Community of Goods." In *Protestant Evangelicalism: Britain, Ireland, Germany and America, 1750-1950: Essays in Honour of W. R. Ward,* edited by Keith Robbins, 25-50. Studies in Church History, Subsidia 7. Oxford: Blackwell, 1990.

3570    Ward, Alfred Dudley. *The Social Creed of the Methodist Church.* Revised edition. Nashville: Abingdon Press, 1965.

3571    Wesley, John. "The Danger of Riches" (1781). Sermon 87 in *The Works of John Wesley, Bicentennial Edition,* 3:227-246.

3572    ———. "The Nature, Design, and General Rules of the United Societies" (1743).

3573 ———. "The Good Steward" (1768). Sermon 51 in *The Works of John Wesley, Bicentennial Edition*, 2:281-298.

3574 ———. "The Reformation of Manners" (1763). Sermon 52 in *The Works of John Wesley, Bicentennial Edition*, 2:300-323.

3575 ———. "Thoughts Upon the Present Scarcity of Provisions" (1773). In *The Works of John Wesley*, edited by Thomas Jackson, 11:53-59.

3576 ———. "The Use of Money" (1760). Sermon 50 in *The Works of John Wesley, Bicentennial Edition*, 2:263-282. Also in *John Wesley*, edited by Albert C. Outler, 238-250; see 4050.

3577 *When the Church Speaks: A Guide to the Social Principles of The United Methodist Church*. Nashville: United Methodist Publishing House, 1996.

## C. Sunday-schools: See Part III, Section 12: Christian Education.

## 32. Spirituality
*See also Part III, Section 14: Class Meetings, and Section 34: Worship.*

3578 Baker, Frank, ed. *The Heart of True Spirituality: John Wesley's Own Choice*. 2 vols. Grand Rapids, Michigan: Francis Asbury Press of Zondervan Publishing House, 1985-1986. Vol. 1: *Selections from William Law*; vol. 2: *Selections from Thomas à Kempis, Pierre Poiret, Jean Duvergier de Hauranne, and Jacques Joseph Duguet*.

3579 Bondi, Roberta C. *In Ordinary Time: Healing the Wounds of the Heart*. Nashville: Abingdon Press, 1996.

3580 ———. *Memories of God: Theological Reflections on a Life*. Nashville: Abingdon Press, 1994.

3581 Bowyer, O. Richard, et al. *Prayer in the Black Tradition*. Nashville: Abingdon Press, 1986.

3582 Clapper, Gregory. *As if the Heart Mattered: A Wesleyan Spirituality*. Nashville: Discipleship Resources, 1997.

3583 Day, Albert E. *Discipline and Discovery: Workbook Edition*. Edited by Danny E. Morris. Nashville: The Upper Room, 1977.

3584 Harkness, Georgia. *Prayer and the Common Life*. Nashville: Abingdon-Cokesbury, 1948.

3585 Harper, Steve. *Devotional Life in the Wesleyan Tradition*. Nashville: The Upper Room, 1983.

3586 ———. *The Devotional Life of John Wesley, 1703-1738*. Doctoral dissertation, Duke University, 1981.

3587 Heitzenrater, Richard P. "The Meditative Piety of the Oxford Methodists" In his *Mirror and Memory: Reflections on Early Methodism*, 78-105; see 3027.

3588   Job, Reuben P. *A Guide to Retreat for All God's Shepherds*. Nashville: Abingdon Press, 1994.

3589   ———. *A Wesleyan Spirituality Reader*. Nashville: The Upper Room, 1997.

3590   Maas, Robin. *Crucified Love: The Practice of Christian Perfection*. Nashville: Abingdon Press, 1989.

3591   ———. "Wesleyan Spirituality: Accountable Discipleship." In *Spiritual Traditions for the Contemporary Church*, edited by Robin Maas and Gabriel O'Donnell, O.P., 303-331. Nashville: Abingdon Press, 1990.

3592   Outler, Albert C. "Spirit and Spirituality in John Wesley." *Quarterly Review* 8/2 (Summer 1988): 3-18.

3593   Palmer, Phoebe. *Phoebe Palmer: Selected Writings*. Edited by Thomas C. Oden. New York: Paulist Press, 1987.

3594   Saliers, Don E. *Worship and Spirituality*. Revised ed. Akron, OH: OSL Publications, 1996. First published in 1985.

3595   ———. *The Soul in Paraphrase: Prayer and the Religious Affections*. Cleveland: Order of Saint Luke Publications, 1992.

3596   Schneider, A. Gregory. *The Way of the Cross Leads Home: Social Domestication of American Methodism*. Bloomington, IN: Indiana University Press, 1993.

3597   Stewart, Carlyle Fielding, III. *Soul Survivors: An African American Spirituality*. Louisville, KY: Westminster/John Knox, 1997.

3598   Trickett, David. "Spiritual Vision and Discipline in the Early Wesleyan Movement." In *Christian Spirituality: Post-Reformation and Modern*, edited by Louis Dupré and Don E. Saliers, 354-371. New York: Crossroad, 1989.

3599   Vogel, Dwight. *Food for Pilgrims: A Journey with Saint Luke*. Akron, OH: OSL Publications, 1996.

3600   Wakefield, Gordon, ed. *The Fire of Love: The Spirituality of John Wesley*. London: Darton, Longman and Todd, 1976.

3601   ———. *Methodist Devotion: The Spiritual Life in the Methodist Tradition, 1791-1945*. London: Epworth Press, 1966.

3602   Wesley, John. *A Christian Library, Consisting of Extracts from and Abridgements of the Choicest Pieces of Practical Divinity which have been Published in the English Tongue*. 30 vols. London: T. Blanshard, 1819-1827. First published in 50 volumes, 1749-1755. Wesley's prefaces only in *The Works of John Wesley*, edited by Thomas Jackson, 14:220-233.

3603   ———. "A Scheme of Self-Examination used by the First Methodists in Oxford." In *The Works of John Wesley*, edited by Thomas Jackson,

11:521-523. Also in *John and Charles Wesley*, edited by Frank Whaling, 85-87; see 3606.

3604 Wesley, Susanna. *Hearts Aflame: Prayers of Susanna, John and Charles Wesley.* Edited by Michael D. McMullen. London: Triangle, 1995.

3605 *Wesleyan Spirituality in Contemporary Theological Education: A Consultation held October 17-19, 1987.* Nashville: Division of Ordained Ministry, General Board of Higher Education and Ministry, UMC, 1987.

3606 Whaling, Frank, ed. *John and Charles Wesley: Selected Prayers, Hymns, Journal Notes, Sermons, Letters, and Treatises.* New York: Paulist Press. 1981. Classics of Western Spirituality series.


## A. Devotional Guides

3607 *Ecumenical Prayer Cycle: "With God's People."* Geneva: World Council of Churches. Annual guide to prayer in 52 weekly sections. Each part of the world where Christian churches exist is lifted up with a simple map, a brief history of Christianity in that country or region, prayers from their churches' worship life, and a description of what issues Christians are struggling with there.

3608 *For All the Saints: A Calendar of Commemorations for United Methodists.* Edited by Clifton F. Guthrie. Akron, OH: Order of Saint Luke Publications, 1995.

3609 *For the Healing of the Nations: Prayer Handbook.* Peterborough: Methodist Publishing House, 1998ff. Prayers for different parts of the world witness of Methodist Districts in Britain; published annually.

3610 *A Guide to Prayer for All God's People,* by Reuben P. Job and Norman Shawchuck. Nashville: The Upper Room, 1991. Prayer companion to the Common Lectionary.

3611 *A Guide to Prayer for Ministers and Other Servants,* by Reuben P. Job and Norman Shawchuck. Nashville: The Upper Room, 1983. Prayer companion to the Common Lectionary.

3612 *Liberation and Unity.* Princeton, NJ: Consultation on Church Union. Annual COCU Lenten study book.

3613 *Prayer Calendar.* Edited by Sheila Bruton. Cincinnati: Service Center, General Board of Global Ministries, UMC. Daily guidance in prayer for the work and workers of the GBGM. Published annually.

3614 *Seasons Of Life: The 1997 Methodist Companion.* Peterborough, England: Methodist Publishing House. Annual devotional guide.

3615 *The Upper Room Disciplines.* Nashville: The Upper Room. Annual devotional manual.

3616 Wesley, John. "A Collection of Forms of Prayer for Every Day in the

Week" (1733). In *The Works of John Wesley*, edited by Thomas Jackson, 11:203-259.

3617 ————. "A Collection of Prayers for Families" (1745). In *The Works of John Wesley*, edited by Thomas Jackson, 11:237-259.

3618 ————. *The Daily Wesley: Excerpts For Every Day in the Year*. Edited by Donald E. Demaray. Anderson, IN: Bristol House, Ltd., 1994.

3619 ————. *Devotions and Prayers of John Wesley*. Compiled and edited by Donald E. Demaray. Grand Rapids, MI: Baker Book House, 1977. Reprint of the 1957 edition.

3620 ————. *Wesley's Forms of Prayer*. Library of Methodist Classics. Nashville: United Methodist Publishing House, 1992. Facsimile reprint of the 1738 edition.

3621 Wesley, Susanna. *The Prayers of Susanna Wesley*. Edited and arranged by William L. Doughty. Grand Rapids, MI: Zondervan Publishing House, 1984. Reprint of the 1955 edition.

## 33. Women

### A. Great Britain

3622 Brown, Earl Kent. *Women in Mr. Wesley's Methodism*. Lewiston, New York: Edwin Mellen Press, 1983.

3623 Burge, Janet. *Women Preachers in Community*. Peterborough, England: Foundery Press, 1996 (People Called Methodists 12).

3624 Chilcote, Paul W. *John Wesley and the Women Preachers of Early Methodism*. ATLA Monograph Series No. 25. Metuchen, NJ: Scarecrow Press, 1991.

3625 ————. *She Offered Them Christ: The Legacy of Women Preachers in Early Methodism*. Nashville: Abingdon Press, 1993.

3626 *A Cry of the Beloved: The Commission on Women Presbyters and the Church*. Peterborough: Methodist Publishing House, 1995. Report to the Methodist Conference, 1995.

3627 Davies, Rupert E. *Methodism and Ministry: The Ministry of Women and Men, Unity and the Future of Methodism*. Peterborough: Methodist Publishing House, 1993.

3628 Field-Bibb, Jacqueline, *Women toward Priesthood: Ministerial Politics and Feminist Praxis*. Cambridge: Cambridge University Press, 1991.

3629 Graham, E. Dorothy. *Chosen by God: The Female Itinerants of Early Primitive Methodism*. Birmingham: Published by the author, 1986. Doctoral dissertation, University of Birmingham, 1986.

3630 Johnson, Dale A. *Women and Religion in Britain and Ireland: An*

*Annotated Bibliography from the Reformation to 1993.* Lanham, MD: Scarecrow Press, 1995.

3631 ———. *Women in English Religion, 1700-1925.* New York: Edwin Mellen Press, 1983.

3632 Leary, William. *Wesley Guild: The First Hundred Years, 1896-1996.* Liverpool: Printed by Mersey Mirror, Ltd, 1995.

3633 Lloyd, Gareth. *Sources for Women's Studies in the Methodist Archives.* Manchester: Methodist Archives & Research Centre, John Rylands University Library, 1996.

3634 Valenze, Deborah Mary. *Prophetic Sons and Daughters: Female Preaching and Popular Religion in Industrial England.* Princeton, NJ: Princeton University Press, 1985.


## B. Germany

3635 Kraft-Buchmueller, Irene. *Die Frauen in der Anfangszeit der Bischoflichen Methodistenkirche in Deutschland.* Stuttgart: Christliches Verlagshaus, 1992.


## C. North America

*See also Section 26: Missions.*

3636 Born, Ethel W. *By My Spirit: The Story of Methodist Protestant Women in Mission, 1879-1939.* New York: Women's Division, General Board of Global Ministries, UMC, 1990.

3637 Campbell, Barbara. *In the Middle of Tomorrow.* New York: Women's Division, General Board of Global Ministries, UMC, 1975.

3638 Dougherty, Mary Agnes. *My Calling to Fulfill: Deaconesses in The United Methodist Tradition.* New York: Women's Division, General Board of Global Ministries, UMC, 1997. Available from Service Center, GBGM, Cincinnati, OH. The basic work.

3639 ———. "The Social Gospel According to Phoebe: Methodist Deaconesses in the Metropolis." Reprinted in *Perspectives on American Methodism*, chapter 24, 356-370; see 3070.

3640 Eltscher, Susan M., ed. *Women in the Wesleyan and United Methodist Traditions: A Bibliography.* Madison, NJ: General Commission on Archives and History, UMC, 1991.

3641 Fagan, Ann. *This Is Our Song: Employed Women in the United Methodist Tradition.* New York: Women's Division, General Board of Global Ministries, UMC, 1986. A history of the Wesleyan Service Guild.

3642 Gagan, Rosemary. *A Sensitive Independence: Canadian Methodist Women Missionaries in Canada and the Orient, 1881-1925.* Montreal: McGill-Queens University Press, 1992.

3643 Garza, Minerva N. "The Influence of Methodism on Hispanic Women Through Women's Societies." *Methodist History* 34/2 (January 1996): 78-89.

3644 Gifford, Carolyn DeSwarte, ed. *The American Deaconess Movement in the Early Twentieth Century.* New York: Garland Publishing, 1986. Includes Isabelle Horton's *The Burden of the City* (1904) and *The Early History of Deaconess Work and Training Schools for Women in American Methodism* (1911), with an introductory essay by Gifford.

3645 ———, ed. *The Debate in the Methodist Episcopal Church over Laity Rights for Women.* New York: Garland Publishing, 1986. Includes essays by James M. Buckley, George W. Hughey, Alpha J. Kynett, and Willis Palmer, with an introductory essay by Gifford.

3646 ———, ed. *The Defense of Women's Right to Ordination in the Methodist Episcopal Church.* New York: Garland Publishing, 1986. Includes Frances Willard's *Woman in the Pulpit* (1889) and William F. Warren's "The Dual Human Unit: The Relationship of Men and Women According to Sociological Teachings of Holy Scripture" (1894), with an introductory essay by Gifford.

3647 ———. " 'For God and Home and Native Land': The WCTU's Image of Woman in the Late Nineteenth Century." Reprinted in *Perspectives on American Methodism,* chapter 20, 309-321; see 3070.

3648 Gillespie, Joanna Bowen. "The Emerging Voice of the Methodist Woman: The Ladies Repository, 1841-61." Reprinted in *Perspectives on American Methodism,* chapter 15, 248-264; see 3070.

3649 Gorrell, Donald K. "A New Impulse: Progress in Lay Leadership and Service by Women of the United Brethren in Christ and the Evangelical Association, 1870-1910." Reprinted in *Perspectives on American Methodism,* chapter 21, 322-331; see 3070.

3650 ———, ed. *Woman's Rightful Place: Women in United Methodist History.* Dayton, OH: United Theological Seminary, 1980. Reflects the EUB experience.

3651 Hale, Harry, Jr., Morton King and Doris M. Jones. *New Witnesses: United Methodist Clergywomen.* Nashville: Division of Ordained Ministry, General Board of Higher Education and Ministry, UMC, 1980.

3652 Hardesty, Nancy A. *Your Daughters Shall Prophesy: Revivalism and Feminism in the Age of Finney.* Brooklyn, NY: Carlson, 1991.

3653 ———. *Women Called to Witness: Evangelical Feminism in the 19th Century.* Nashville: Abingdon Press, 1984. Brief, popular version of *Your Daughters Shall Prophesy* (above).

3654 Herb, Carol Marie. *The Light Along the Way: A Living History Through*

*United Methodist Women's Magazines.* New York : General Board of Global Ministries, UMC, 1995.

3655 Hill, Patricia R. *The World Their Household: The American Woman's Foreign Mission Movement and Cultural Transformation, 1870-1920.* Ann Arbor, MI: University of Michigan Press, 1985.

3656 Hoover, Theressa. *With Unveiled Face: Centennial Reflections on Women and Men in the Community of the Church.* New York: Women's Division, General Board of Global Ministries, UMC, 1983.

3657 Keller, Rosemary Skinner. "Creating a Sphere for Women: The Methodist Episcopal Church, 1869-1906." Reprinted in *Perspectives on American Methodism,* chapter 22, 332-342; see 3070.

3658 ———. et al., eds. *Methodist Women, A World Sisterhood: A History of the World Federation of Methodist Women.* Cincinnati, OH: World Federation of Methodist Women, 1986.

3659 ———, ed. *Spirituality and Social Responsibility: The Vocational Vision of Women in the Methodist Tradition.* Nashville: Abingdon Press, 1993.

3660 ———, Hilah F. Thomas and Louise L. Queen, eds. *Women in New Worlds: Historical Perspectives on the Wesleyan Tradition.* 2 vols. Nashville: Abingdon Press, 1981-82.

3661 Kim, Ai Ra. *Women Struggling for a New Life: The Role of Religion in the Cultural Passage from Korea to America.* Albany, NY: State University of New York Press, 1996.

3662 Kim, Jung Ha. *Bridge-Makers and Cross-Bearers: Korean American Women and the Church.* Atlanta: Scholars Press, 1995.

3663 Knotts, Alice G. *Fellowship of Love: Methodist Women Changing American Racial Attitudes, 1920-1968.* Nashville: Kingswood Books, 1997.

3664 Kreutziger, Sarah S. *Going on to Perfection: The Contributions of the Wesleyan Doctrine of Entire Sanctification to the Value Base of American Professional Social Work through the Eyes of Nineteenth-Century Evangelical Women Reformers.* Doctoral dissertation, Tulane University, 1991.

3665 Lakey, Othal H. *God in My Mamma's House: A Study of the Women's Movement in the CME Church.* Memphis, TN: C.M.E. Publishing House, 1994.

3666 Lee, Luther. *Woman's Right to Preach the Gospel.* Syracuse, NY: J.E Masters, 1852. Reprinted in Luther Lee's *Five Sermons and a Tract.* Edited by Donald W. Dayton. Chicago: Holrad House, 1975.

3667 Lobody, Diane H. " 'That Language Might Be Given Me': Women's Experience in Early Methodism." Reprinted in *Perspectives On American Methodism,* chapter 8, 127-144; see 3070.

3668 McDowell, John Patrick. *The Social Gospel in the South: The Woman's Home*

*Mission Movement in the Methodist Episcopal Church, South, 1886-1939.* Baton Rouge, LA: Louisiana State University Press, 1982.

3669 McKay, Nellie Y. "Nineteenth-Century Black Women's Spiritual Auto-biographies: Religious Faith and Self-Empowerment." Reprinted in *Perspectives on American Methodism*, chapter 11, 178-191; see 3070.

3670 Myers, Sarah Joyce. *Southern Methodist Women Leaders and Church Missions, 1878-1910.* Doctoral dissertation, Emory University, 1990.

3671 Muir, Elizabeth. *Petticoats in the Pulpit: The Story of Early Nineteenth Century Methodist Women Preachers in Upper Canada.* Toronto: United Church Publishing House, 1991.

3672 Oehler, Carolyn Henninger. *The Journey Is Our Home: A History of the General Commission on the Status and Role of Women.* Evanston: GCOS-ROW, 1996.

3673 Palmer, Phoebe. *The Promise of the Father; or, A Neglected Speciality of the Last Days.* Salem, OH: Schmul Publishers, 1981. Reprint of the 1859 edition; also reprinted New York: Garland Publishing, 1985. A massive defense of women's right to preach based on the promise of Joel 2:28.

3674 Reber, Audrie. *Women United in Mission: A History of the Woman's Society of World Service of the Evangelical United Brethren Church, 1946-1968.* Dayton, OH: Otterbein Press, 1969. Available from Service Center, General Board of Global Ministries, UMC, Cincinnati, OH.

3675 Roberts, Benjamin T. *Ordaining Women.* Indianapolis, IN: Light and Life Press, 1992. Reprint of the 1891 edition.

3676 Rowe, Kenneth E. "Ordination of Women, Round One: Anna Oliver and the Methodist General Conference of 1880." *Methodist History,* 12 (April 1974): 60-72. Reprinted in *Perspectives on American Methodism*, chapter 19, 298-308; see 3070.

3677 Schmidt, Jean Miller. *Grace Sufficient: A History of Women in American Methodism.* Nashville: Abingdon Press, 1999. Forthcoming.

3678 Stanley, Susie C. *Wesleyan/Holiness Women Clergy: A Preliminary Bibliography.* Portland, OR: Western Evangelical Seminary, 1994.

3679 Stevens, Thelma. *Legacy for the Future: The History of Christian Social Relations in the Woman's Division of Christian Service, 1940- 1968.* Cincinnati: Women's Division, General Board of Global Ministries, UMC, 1978.

3680 Sweet, Leonard I. *The Minister's Wife: Her Role in Nineteenth-Century American Evangelicalism.* Philadephia: Temple University Press, 1983.

3681 *To a Higher Glory: The Growth and Development of Black Women Organized for Mission in the Methodist Church, 1940-1968.* Cincinnati: Board of Global Ministries, UMC, 1978.

3682 United Methodist Women. *Handbook for United Methodist Women:*

*Focus on Local Units, 1997-2000.* New York: Women's Division, General Board of Global Ministries, UMC, 1996.

3683 Willard, Frances. *Woman in the Pulpit.* Boston: D. Lothrop Co., 1888. See Carolyn D. Gifford, *Defense of Women's Right to Ordination*; see 3646.

3684 *Words That Hurt and Words That Heal: Language about God and People.* New edition. Nashville: Graded Press, 1991. Leader's guide plus full text of document prepared in 1988 by the United Methodist Task Force on Language Guidelines.

## 34. Worship

### A. Service Books: Caribbean

3685 *The Prayer Book of the Methodist Church.* Peterborough: Methodist Publishing House, on behalf of the Methodist Church in the Caribbean and the Americas, 1992.

### B. Service Books: England

3686 *Draft Services for Trial Use and Comment.* Peterborough: Methodist Publishing House, 1994-96. Part of the process of preparing a sucessor to the following item.

3687 *The Methodist Service Book.* London: Methodist Publishing House, 1992. Revised and expanded version of 1975 edition.

### C. Service Books: Germany

3688 *Agende der Evangelisch-Methodistischen Kirche.* Stuttgart: Christliches Verlagshaus, 1991.

3689 *Feiern und Bekennen: Ordnungen, Gebete, und Bekenntnisse fur den Gottesdienst in der Evangelisch-Methodistischen Kirche.* Stuttgart: Christliches Verlagshaus, 1994. Abridged and revised version of *Agende 1991* for the people in the pew.

3690 *Liturgie der Evangelisch-Methodistischen Kirche.* Zurich: Verlag CVB Buch & Druck, 1981.

### D. Service Books: Korea

3691 Korean Methodist Church. *The Book of Worship [Kidokyo Taehnan Kamnihoi Yebaeso].* Seoul: Department of Mission of the Korean Methodist Church, 1992.

## E. Service Books: United States

### African Methodist Episcopal Church
3692　*The Book of Worship*. Nashville: A.M.E. Sunday School Union, 1984.

### African Methodist Episcopal Zion Church
3693　*Book of Worship*. Charlotte, NC: A.M.E. Zion Publishing House, 1997.

### Christian Methodist Episcopal Church
3694　*Book of Ritual*. Memphis, TN: C.M.E. Publishing House, 1995.

### Church of the Nazarene
3695　*The Church Rituals Handbook*.Compiled by Jesse C. Middendorf. Kansas City: Beacon Hill Press, 1997.

### Free Methodist Church
3696　*Pastor's Handbook*. Edited by Clyde E. Van Valin. 3d ed. Indianapolis, IN: Light and Life Press, 1991.

### The United Methodist Church
3697　*The Book of Offices and Services after the Usage of the Order of Saint Luke*. Cleveland: Order of Saint Luke Publishing Office, 1988.
3698　*Ceremonies III: A Collection of Worship Resources for United Methodist Women*. New York: Women's Division, General Board of Global Ministries, UMC, 1996.
3699　*The Daily Office, a Book of Hours for Daily Prayer*. 4 vols. Cleveland: Order of Saint Luke Publications, 1991-1994. Vol. 1, *Advent, Christmas, Epiphany, Baptism of our Lord*; Vol. 2, *Lent through Easter Vigil*; Vol. 3, *Easter Vigil through the Great Fifty Days*; Vol. 4, *Trinity through Christ the King*.
3700　*For All the Saints: A Calendar of Commemorations for United Methodists*. Edited by Clifton F. Guthrie. Akron, OH: Order of Saint Luke Publications, 1995.
3701　*The New Handbook of the Christian Year*. Edited by Hoyt C. Hickman, et al. Second edition. Nashville: Abingdon Press, 1992.
3702　*John Wesley's Prayer Book: The Sunday Service of the Methodists in North America*. With introduction, notes, and commentary by James F. White. Cleveland: Order of Saint Luke Publications, 1992.
3703　*Lift Up Your Hearts: Eucharistic Prayers Based on the Common Lectionary*. Edited by Michael J. O'Donnell. 3 vols. Cleveland: OSL Publications, 1989-1991. The Prayers of Great Thanksgiving patterned after those

found in *The United Methodist Hymnal* 1989, with segments based on the texts of the Common Lectionary, Year A, B, and C.

3704    *To Remember and Celebrate: Worship Resources for Heritage Events.* Madison, NJ : General Commission on Archives & History, UMC, 1995.

3705    *The United Methodist Book of Worship.* Nashville: United Methodist Publishing House, 1992. Software edition Windows 3.5" available.

3706    *The United Methodist Hymnal: Book of United Methodist Worship.* Nashville: United Methodist Publishing House, 1989.

3707    *The United Methodist Music & Worship Planner, 1996-1997.* Nashville: Abingdon Press, 1996. Published annually.

3708    *The Upper Room Worshipbook: Music and Liturgies for Spiritual Formation.* Nashville: The Upper Room, 1985.

## Wesleyan Church

3709    *Wesleyan Pastor's Manual.* 4th ed. Indianapolis: Wesleyan Publishing House, 1996.

## F. History and Commentary: Global

3710    Tucker, Karen Westerfield, ed. *The Sunday Service of the Methodists: Twentieth-Century Worship in Worldwide Methodism, Studies in Honor of James F. White.* Nashville: Kingswood Books, 1995.

## G. History and Commentary: England

3711    Baker, Frank. *Methodism and the Love Feast.* London: Epworth Press, 1957.

3712    Burdon, Adrian. *The Preaching Service, The Glory of the Methodists: A Study of the Piety, Ethos and Development of the Methodist Preaching Service.* Bramcote, England: Grove Books, 1991.

3713    Davies, Horton. *Worship and Theology in England*, 6 volumes in 3. Grand Rapids, MI : Eerdmans, 1996. See especially 3:143-209. Reprint of the 1961 edition, with additional volume on the second half of the twentieth century.

3714    Kimbrough, S. T., ed. "Worship in Eighteenth Century Anglicanism and Methodism." *Proceedings of the Charles Wesley Society* I (1994): 1-135.

3715    Tucker, Karen B. Westerfield. "John Wesley's Prayer Book Revision: The Text in Context." *Methodist History* 34 (July 1996): 230- 247.

3716    White, Susan J. *Groundwork of Christian Worship.* London: Epworth Press, 1997.

## H. History and Commentary: Germany

*See Walter F. Klaiber article in 3710.*

3717 Marquardt, Manfred, Dieter Sackmann and David Tripp, eds. *Theologie des Gotteslobs*. Stuttgart: Christliches Verlagshaus, 1991.

## I. History and Commentary: United States

3718 Costen, Melva Wilson. *African American Christian Worship*. Nashville: Abingdon Press, 1993.

3719 Elkins, Heather M. *Living on Borrowed Time: The Christian Calendar in 20th Century United Methodism*. Doctoral dissertation, Drew University, 1991.

3720 ———. *Worshiping Women: Re-Forming God's People for Praise*. Nashville: Abingdon Press, 1995.

3721 González, Justo L., ed. *Alabadle: Hispanic Christian Worship*. Nashville: Abingdon Press, 1996. Chapter 4, "Worship in the Hispanic United Methodist Church," by Maria Luisa Santillan Baert, 57-72.

3722 Harmon, Nolan B. *The Rites and Ritual of Episcopal Methodism*. Nashville: Parthenon Press, 1996. Reprint of 1926 edition.

3723 Hickman, Hoyt L. *Worship Resources of The United Methodist Hymnal: Introduction to the General Services, Psalter and Other Acts of Worship*. Nashville : Abingdon Press, 1989.

3724 ———. *Worshiping with United Methodists: A Guide for Pastors and Worship Leaders*. Nashville: Abingdon Press, 1996. The basic work.

3725 McClain, William B. *Come Sunday: The Liturgy of Zion*. Nashville: Abingdon Press, 1990.

3726 Peiffer, Robert B. *How Contemporary Liturgies Evolve: The Revision of United Methodist Liturgical Texts, 1968-1988*. Doctoral dissertation, University of Notre Dame, 1993.

3727 Procter-Smith, Marjorie. *In Her Own Rite: Constructing Feminist Liturgical Tradition*. Nashville: Abingdon Press, 1990.

3728 ———. *Praying With Our Eyes Open: Engendering Feminist Liturgical Prayer*. Nashville: Abingdon Press, 1996.

3729 Ruth, Lester W. *"A Little Heaven Below": Quarterly Meetings as Seasons of Grace in Early American Methodism*. Doctoral dissertation, University of Notre Dame, 1996.

3730 Stookey, Lawrence Hull. *Calendar: Christ's Time for the Church*. Nashville: Abingdon Press, 1996.

3731 Taylor, David L. "The Order of St. Luke and *The Versicle*: A Résumé, 1946-1961." *Doxology* 3 (1986): 48-56.

3732 Tucker, Karen Westerfield. *"Till Death Us Do Part": The Rites of Marriage and Burial Prepared by John Wesley and Their Development in the Methodist*

*Episcopal Church.* Doctoral dissertation, University of Notre Dame, 1992.

3733 Wade, William N. *A History of Public Worship in the Methodist Episcopal Church and the Methodist Episcopal Church, South, from 1784 to 1905.* Doctoral dissertation, University of Notre Dame, 1981.

3734 Wainwright, Geoffrey. *Worship with One Accord: Where Liturgy and Ecumenism Embrace.* New York: Oxford University Press, 1997.

3735 White, James F. *Protestant Worship: Traditions in Transition.* Louisville: Westminster/John Knox Press, 1989. Chapter 9, "Methodist Worship," reprinted in *Perspectives on American Methodism*, chapter 31, 460-479; see 3070. The best brief survey.


## 35. Youth

3736 Blount, Emanuel Lee. *The History of the Epworth League: A Concept of Youth in Nineteenth Century America.* Doctoral dissertation, State University of New York, Buffalo, 1996.

3737 Hutchinson, Paul. *The Story of the Epworth League.* Cincinnati: Methodist Book Concern, 1927.

3738 Smith, J. Warren. "Youth Ministry in American Methodism's Mission." *Methodist History* 19/4 (July 1981): 224-230.

# PART IV: DOCTRINE

*For publications issued after December 1997, plus a large section on "Representative Methodist Theologians through 1997" arranged chronologically and a section on Methodist Biblical studies deleted from this edition, consult UM Studies: Basic Bibliographies at www.gcah.org.*

## 1. Basic Doctrinal Statements of The United Methodist Church

4001  *The Book of Discipline of The United Methodist Church*, 1996. Nashville: United Methodist Publishing House, 1996. Part II: "Doctrinal Standards and Our Theological Task," 60-63.

4002  *Doctrinal Standards and Our Theological Task*. Nashville: United Methodist Publishing House, 1988. Reprint of Part II of the *Discipline*, with leader's guide by Kenneth L. Carder.

## 2. Basic Doctrinal Statements of the Methodist Church (Great Britain)

4003  *Constitutional Practice and Discipline of the Methodist Church*. Peterborough: Methodist Publishing House, 1988- . Vol. 1, Historical documents amended by Act of Parliament only; first published in 1951, 7th edition, 1988. Vol. 2, Standing orders, updated annually.

4004  *The Faith and Order Statements of Methodism, 1933-1983*. Peterborough: Methodist Publishing House, 1984.

4005  *Called to Love and Praise: The Methodist Church Faith and Order Committee Report to Conference 1995*. Peterborough: Methodist Publishing House, 1995.

## 3. Contemporary Discussions of Basic Methodist Doctrines (UMC)

4006  Abraham, William J. *Waking from Doctrinal Amnesia: The Healing of Doctrine in The United Methodist Church*. Nashville : Abingdon Press, 1995.

4007  Campbell, Dennis M. et al, eds. *Doctrines and Discipline: Methodist Theology and Practice*. Nashville: Abingdon Press, 1999. United Methodism and American Culture series.

4008   Carder, Kenneth L. *Living Our Beliefs: The United Methodist Way.* Nashville: Discipleship Resources, 1996.

4009   ———.*Who Are We? Doctrine, Ministry and Mission of The United Methodist Church.* Nashville: Abingdon Press, 1997. Student book and leader's guide.

4010   Cobb, John B. *Grace and Responsibility: A Wesleyan Theology for Today.* Nashville: Abingdon Press, 1995.

4011   *Foundations: Shaping the Ministry of Christian Education in Your Congregation.* Nashville: Discipleship Resources, 1993.

4012   Heidinger, James V., ed. *Basic United Methodist Beliefs: An Evangelical View.* Wilmore, KY: Bristol Books, 1986.

4013   Langford, Thomas A., ed. *Doctrine and Theology in The United Methodist Church.* Nashville: Kingswood Books, 1990. Sets 1972 and 1988 doctrinal statements in historical context.

4014   Meeks, M. Douglas, ed. *What Should Methodists Teach? Wesleyan Tradition and Modern Diversity.* Nashville: Kingswood Books, 1990.

4015   Outler, Albert C. *Theology in the Wesleyan Spirit.* Nashville: Discipleship Resources, 1975.

4016   Runyon, Theodore H., ed. *Wesleyan Theology Today: A Bicentennial Theological Consultation.* Nashville: Kingswood Books, 1985.

4017   Thorsen, Donald A. *The Wesleyan Quadrilateral: Scripture, Tradition, Reason & Experience as a Model of Evangelical Theology.* Grand Rapids, MI: Francis Asbury Press of Zondervan Publishing House, 1990.

## 4. John and Charles Wesley

### A. Bibliography
4018   Baker, Frank. *A Union Catalogue of the Publications of John and Charles Wesley.* Carbondale, PA: George Zimmermann, 1991. Reprint of the 1966 edition.

4019   Green, Richard. *The Works of John and Charles Wesley.* 2nd revised edition. New York: AMS Press, 1976. Reprint of the 1906 edition.

4020   Jarboe, Betty M. *John and Charles Wesley: A Bibliography.* Metuchen, NJ: Scarecrow Press, 1987.

### B. Basic Texts

#### Charles Wesley
4021   *Charles Wesley: A Reader.* Compiled by John R. Tyson. New York: Oxford University Press, 1989.

4022   *Charles Wesley's Earliest Sermons.* Edited by Thomas A. Albin and Oliver

A. Beckerlegge. London: Wesley Historical Society, 1987. Six unpublished manuscript sermons.

4023 *The Journal of the Rev. Charles Wesley.* Edited by Thomas Jackson. 2 vols. London: John Mason, 1949; reprinted Grand Rapids, MI: Baker Book House, 1980.

4024 *Poetical Works of John and Charles Wesley.* Edited by George Osborn. London: Wesleyan Conference Office, 1872. 13 vols.

4025 *The Unpublished Poetical Writings of Charles Wesley.* Edited by S. T. Kimbrough, Jr., and Oliver A. Beckerlegge. 3 vols. Nashville: Kingswood Books, 1988-1992.

## Charles Wesley Society reprint series:
4026 *Hymns for the Nativity of Our Lord* (1991)
4027 *Hymns for our Lord's Resurrection* (1992)
4028 *Ascension-Day and Whitsunday Hymns* (1994)
4029 *Hymns on the Lord's Supper* (1995). One hundred sixty-six eucharistic hymns with Wesley's extract from Daniel Brevint's *Christian Sacrament and Sacrifice* (1673). Facsimile reprint of the 1745 edition, with introduction by Geoffrey Wainwright.
4030 *Hymns on the Great Festivals* (1996). Wesley texts and tunes by John Lampe; introduction, notes and tune realizations by Frank Baker, Robin A. Leaver, and Carlton R. Young. See also 3606.

## John Wesley
4031 *Explanatory Notes upon the New Testament.* Nashville: Parthenon Press, 1996.
4032 *Explanatory Notes upon the Old Testament.* 3 vols. Bristol: William Pine, 1765. Facsimile reprint, Salem, OH: Schmul Publishers, 1975. A convenient one-volume reprint of both Old and New Testaments Notes is *Wesley's Notes on the Bible,* edited by G. Roger Schoenhals. Grand Rapids, MI: Francis Asbury Press of Zondervan Publishing House, 1987.
4033 *John Wesley's Sermons: An Anthology.* Edited by Albert C. Outler and Richard P. Heitzenrater. Nashville: Abingdon Press, 1991.
4034 *The Journal of the Rev. John Wesley.* Edited by Nehemiah Curnock. 8 vols. London: Epworth Press, 1909-1916. The standard annotated edition of the *Journal;* being replaced by the *Bicentennial Edition* of the *Journal and Diaries,* edited by W. Reginald Ward and Richard P. Heitzenrater; see 4043.
4035 *The Letters of the Rev. John Wesley.* Edited by John Telford. 8 vols. London: Epworth Press, 1931. The standard annotated edition of the *Letters;* being replaced by the much expanded and more accurate *Bicentennial Edition* of the *Letters,* edited by Frank Baker; see 4044.

4036 *Obras de Wesley*. Editor general Justo L. González. Edicion auspiciada por Wesley Heritage Foundation. Franklin, TN: Providence House Publishers, 1996. v. 1-4 Sermons, v. 5 Las Primeras Sociedades Metodistas,v. 6 Defensa del Metodismo.

4037 *A Plain Account of Christian Perfection*. London: Epworth Press; Philadelphia: Trinity Press International, 1990.

4038 *The Works of John Wesley*. Begun as *The Oxford Edition of the Works of John Wesley* (Oxford: Clarendon Press, 1975-1983); continued as *The Bicentennial Edition of the Works of John Wesley* (Nashville: Abingdon Press, 1984–). All volumes in print are now available from Abingdon Press; referred to in these bibliographies as *Bicentennial Edition*. Projected to be 35 volumes; editors and dates given below are for published volumes only.

4039 Vol. 1-4: *Sermons*. Edited by Albert C. Outler (1984-1987).

4040 Vol. 7: *A Collection of Hymns for the Use of the People Called Methodists (1780)*. Edited by Franz Hildebrandt and Oliver Beckerlegge (1983).

4041 Vol. 9: *The Methodist Societies I: History, Nature and Design*. Edited by Rupert E. Davies (1989).

4042 Vol. 11: *The Appeals To Men of Reason and Religion and Certain Related Open Letters*. Edited by Gerald R. Cragg (1975).

4043 Vol. 18-24: *Journal and Diaries*. Edited by W. Reginald Ward and Richard P. Heitzenrater (1988-1998).

4044 Vol. 25-26: *Letters*. Edited by Frank Baker (1980–).

4045 *The Works of the Rev. John Wesley*. Edited by Thomas Jackson. 14 vols. London: Wesleyan Methodist Book Room, 1829-1831. Reprinted Grand Rapids, MI: Baker Book House, 1978. Has for years been the standard edition of Wesley's *Works*; now being replaced by the *Bicentennial Edition*; see 4038.

4046 *The Works of John Wesley* on CD-ROM. Produced by Segen Corporation in conjunction with Providence House Publishers, Nashville, 1995. Electronic version of Jackson edition text frees you from needing a separate concordance or index to search for key words and phrases, and allows you to export portions of texts directly into a word processing file and print hard copies. One disc. System requirements: compatible with Windows 3.1 and higher; Macintosh system 7 and higher (68020 minimum processor), including Power Macintosh. Can be networked for additional fee. Order from Cokesbury or directly from Segen Corporation, 108 Crosspointe, Hendersonville, TN 37075. 1-800-737-0877/ FAX 1-615-822-8458/online: www.segen/wesley/product.htm.

## C. Selections

4047      Burtner, Robert W. and Robert E. Chiles, eds. *John Wesley's Theology: A Collection from His Works*. Nashville: Abingdon Press, 1982. Reprint of the 1954 edition entitled *A Compend of Wesley's Theology.*

4048      Jarboe, Betty M., comp. *Wesley Quotations: Excerpts from the Writings of John Wesley and Other Family Members*. Metuchen, NJ: Scarecrow Press, 1990.

4049      Jay, Elisabeth, ed. *The Journal of John Wesley: A Selection*. New York: Oxford University Press, 1987.

4050      Outler, Albert C., ed. *John Wesley*. (The Library of Protestant Thought) New York: Oxford University Press, 1964.

4051      Watson, Philip S., ed. *The Message of the Wesleys: A Reader*. Grand Rapids, MI: Zondervan Publishing House, 1984. Reprint of 1964 edition.

4052      Whaling, Frank, ed. *John and Charles Wesley: Selected Prayers, Hymns, Journal Notes, Sermons, Letters and Treatises*. Classics of Western Spirituality. New York: Paulist Press, 1981.

## D. Biographies of John and Charles Wesley

*For historical context, see Part III, Section 1.*

4053      Gill, Frederick C. *Charles Wesley, the First Methodist*. London: Lutterworth Press, 1964.

4054      Green, V. H. H. *John Wesley*. Lanham, MD: University Press of America, 1987. Reprint of 1964 edition.

4055      Heitzenrater, Richard P. *The Elusive Mr. Wesley*. 2 vols. Nashville: Parthenon Press, 1996. Reprint of the 1984 edition.

4056      ———. *Mirror and Memory: Reflections on Early Methodism*. Nashville: Kingswood Books, 1989.

4057      ———. *Wesley and the People Called Methodists*. Nashville: Abingdon Press, 1995. The basic work.

4058      McEllhenney, John G. *John Wesley: A Man Who Shook the Spiritual Earth*. Madison, NJ: General Commission on Archives & History, 1996. Best brief sketch.

4059      Pudney, John. *John Wesley and His World*. New York: Charles Scribner's Sons, 1978. Readable text, plus 125 excellent illustrations.

4060      Rack, Henry D. *Reasonable Enthusiast: John Wesley and the Rise of Methodism*. Revised edition. Nashville: Abingdon Press, 1993.

## E. Theological Interpretations

4061      Baker, Frank. *Charles Wesley's Verse: An Introduction*. 2nd edition. London: Epworth Press, 1988.

4062      Campbell, Ted A. *John Wesley and Christian Antiquity: Religious Vision and Cultural Change*. Nashville: Kingswood Books, 1991.

4063    Cannon, William R. *The Theology of John Wesley, with Special Reference to the Doctrine of Justification.* Lanham, MD: University Press of America, 1984. Reprint of the 1946 edition.

4064    Cell, George C. *The Rediscovery of John Wesley.* Lanham, MD: University Press of America, 1984. Reprint of 1935 edition.

4065    Clapper, Gregory S. *John Wesley on Religious Affections: His Views on Experience and Emotion and Their Role in the Christian Life and Theology.* Metuchen, NJ: Scarecrow Press, 1989.

4066    Clifford, Alan C. *Atonement and Justification. English Evangelical Theology, 1640-1790: An Evaluation.* Oxford: Clarendon Press, 1990.

4067    Collins, Kenneth J. *The Scripture Way of Salvation: The Heart of Wesley's Theology.* Nashville: Abingdon Press, 1997.

4068    Coppedge, Allan. *John Wesley in Theological Debate.* Wilmore, KY: Wesley Heritage Press, 1988.

4069    Deschner, John. *Wesley's Christology: An Interpretation.* Dallas: Southern Methodist University Press, 1985. Reprint of 1960 edition with a new foreword by the author.

4070    Gunter, W. Stephen. *The Limits of "Love Divine": John Wesley's Response to Antinomianism and Enthusiasm.* Nashville: Kingswood Books, 1989.

4071    ———, et al. *Wesley and the Quadrilateral: Renewing the Conversation.* Nashville: Abingdon Press, 1997.

4072    Hildebrandt, Franz. *Christianity According to the Wesleys.* Grand Rapids, MI: Baker Books, 1997. Reprint of 1956 edition.

4073    Jennings, Theodore W., Jr. *Good News to the Poor: John Wesley's Evangelical Economics.* Nashville: Abingdon Press, 1990.

4074    Jones, Scott J. *John Wesley's Concept and Use of Scripture.* Nashville: Kingswood Books, 1995.

4075    Kimbrough, S. T., Jr., ed. *Charles Wesley: Poet and Theologian.* Nashville: Kingswood Books, 1992.

4076    Knight, Henry H., III. *The Presence of God in the Christian Life: John Wesley and the Means of Grace.* Lanham, MD: Scarecrow Press, 1992.

4077    Lindström, Harald. *Wesley and Sanctification: A Study in the Doctrine of Salvation.* Grand Rapids, MI: Francis Asbury Press of Zondervan Publishing House, 1982. Reprint of 1950 edition.

4078    Maddox, Randy L. *Responsible Grace: John Wesley's Practical Theology.* Nashville: Kingswood Books, 1994. Best comprehensive study.

4079    Monk, Robert C. *John Wesley: His Puritan Heritage.* Revised edition. Nashville: Abingdon Press, 1998. Forthcoming. Revision of 1966 edition.

4080    Naglee, David I. *From Everlasting to Everlasting: John Wesley on Eternity and Time.* 2 vols. New York: Peter Lang, 1991-1992.

4081    Oden, Thomas C. *Wesley's Teaching.* 3 vols. Grand Rapids, MI: Zondervan Publishing House, 1992-1994. Forthcoming. Vol. 1: *Systematic Theology*; vol. 2: *Pastoral Care*; vol. 3: *Ethics and Society*.

4082 Outler, Albert C. *The Wesleyan Theological Heritage: Essays of Albert C. Outler.* Edited by Thomas C. Oden and Leicester R. Longden. Grand Rapids, MI: Francis Asbury Press of Zondervan Publishing House, 1991.

4083 ———. *Theology in the Wesleyan Spirit.* Nashville: Discipleship Resources, 1975.

4084 Rowe, Kenneth E., ed. *The Place of Wesley in the Christian Tradition.* Revised edition. Metuchen, NJ: Scarecrow Press, 1980. Reissue of 1976 edition with updated bibliography.

4085 Runyon, Theodore H. *The New Creation: John Wesley's Theology Today.* Nashville: Abingdon Press, 1998.

4086 Sangster, William E. *The Path to Perfection: An Examination and Restatement of John Wesley's Doctrine of Christian Perfection.* London: Epworth Press, 1984. Reprint of 1943 edition.

4087 Schmidt, Martin. *John Wesley: A Theological Biography.* 2 vols. in 3. Nashville: Abingdon Press, 1962-1973.

4088 Stacey, John, ed. *John Wesley: Contemporary Perspectives.* London: Epworth Press, 1988.

4089 Starkey, Lycurgus M., Jr. *The Work of the Holy Spirit: A Study in Wesleyan Theology.* Nashville: Parthenon Press, 1996. Reprint of the 1962 edition.

4090 Tuttle, Robert G., Jr. *Mysticism in the Wesleyan Tradition.* Grand Rapids, MI: Francis Asbury Press of Zondervan Publishing House, 1989.

4091 Tyson, John R. *Charles Wesley on Sanctification: A Biographical and Theological Study.* Grand Rapids, MI: Francis Asbury Press of Zondervan Publishing House, 1986.

4092 Yrigoyen, Charles. *John Wesley: Holiness of Heart and Life.* New York: Women's Division, General Board of Global Ministries, UMC, 1996. Best beginner's guide.

## 5. History of Doctrine
*For the Holiness Movement, see Part III, Section 23.*

4093 Baker, Frank. "The Doctrines in the Discipline." In his *From Wesley to Asbury: Studies in Early American Methodism*, 162-182. Durham, NC: Duke University Press, 1976. Reprinted in *Perspectives on American Methodism*, chapter 3, 46-61; see 3070.

4094 Chiles, Robert E. *Theological Transition in American Methodism, 1790-*

*1935*. Lanham, MD: University Press of America, 1984. Reprint of the 1965 edition.

4095     Cushman, Robert E. *John Wesley's Experimental Divinity: Studies in Methodist Doctrinal Standards*. Nashville: Kingswood Books, 1989.

4096     Deats, Paul and Carol Robb, eds. *The Boston Personalist Tradition in Philosophy, Social Ethics, and Theology*. Macon, GA: Mercer University Press, 1986.

4097     Dunlap, E. Dale. *Methodist Theology in Great Britain in the 19th Century, with Special Reference to the Theology of Adam Clarke, Richard Watson, and William Burt Pope*. Doctoral dissertation, Yale University, 1956. Ann Arbor, MI: University Microfilms, 1968.

4098     Heitzenrater, Richard P. "At Full Liberty: Doctrinal Standards in Early American Methodism." In his *Mirror and Memory: Reflections on Early Methodism*, 189-204. Nashville: Kingswood Books, 1989. Reprinted in *Perspectives on American Methodism*, chapter 4, 62-76; see 3070.

4099     Holifield, E. Brooks. *The Gentlemen Theologians: American Theology in Southern Culture*. Durham, NC: Duke University Press, 1978. See especially 76-77, 140-143, 165- 169, 186-202.

4100     Jones, Smith Jameson. *Three Representative Leaders in Contemporary American Methodist Theology*. Doctoral dissertation, Vanderbilt University, 1965. A study of Knudson, Lewis and Rall.

4101     Langford, Thomas A., ed. *Doctrine and Theology in The United Methodist Church*. Nashville: Kingswood Books, 1990. Sets 1972 and 1988 doctrinal statements in historical context.

4102     ———. *Practical Divinity*. Revised edition. Nashville: Abingdon Press, 1998. Vol. 1: *Theology in the Wesleyan Tradition*; vol. 2, *Readings in Wesleyan Theology*. Revision of 1983-84 set. The basic survey with selected readings from primary sources.

4103     McCutcheon, William J. "American Methodist Thought and Theology, 1919-1960." In *History of American Methodism*, edited by Emory S. Bucke, 3:261-327; see 3056.

4104     ———. *Essays in American Theology: The Life and Thought of Harris Franklin Rall*. New York: Philosophical Library, 1973.

4105     Naumann, William H. *Theology and German-American Evangelicalism: The Role of Theology in the Church of the United Brethren in Christ and the Evangelical Association*. Doctoral dissertation, Yale University, 1966.

4106     Norwood, Frederick A., ed. *The Methodist Discipline of 1798, Including the Annotations of Thomas Coke and Francis Asbury*. Rutland, VT: Academy Books, 1979.

4107     Oden, Thomas C. *Doctrinal Standards in the Wesleyan Tradition*. Grand Rapids, MI: Francis Asbury Press of Zondervan Publishing House, 1988.

4108   Outler, Albert C. *The Wesleyan Theological Heritage: Essays of Albert C. Outler.* Edited by Thomas C. Oden and Leicester R. Longden. Grand Rapids, MI: Francis Asbury Press of Zondervan Publishing House, 1991.

4109   Peters, John L. *Christian Perfection and American Methodism.* Nashville: Parthenon Press, 1996. Reprint of the 1956 edition with a new foreword by Albert C. Outler.

4110   Runyon, Theodore H., ed. *Wesleyan Theology Today: A Bicentennial Theological Consultation.* Nashville: Kingswood Books, 1985.

4111   *Sanctification in the Benedictine and Methodist Traditions: A World Ecumenical Conference Held in Rome, July 4-10, 1994.* Special issue, *Asbury Theological Journal* 50/2, 51/1 (Fall 1995/Spring 1996).

4112   Seamands, Stephen A. *Christology and Transition in the Theology of Edwin Lewis.* Lanham, MD: University Press of America, 1987.

4113   Scott, Leland. "The Concern for Systematic Theology, 1840-1870." In *History of American Methodism*, edited by Emory S. Bucke, 2:380-390; see 3056. Reprinted in *Perspectives on American Methodism*, chapter 17, 277-288; see 3070.

4114   ———. "The Message of Early American Methodism." In *History of American Methodism*, edited by Emory S. Bucke, 1:291-359; see 3059.

4115   ———. "Methodist Theology in America in the 19th Century." *Religion in Life* 25 (Winter 1955-1956): 87-98.

4116   ———. *Methodist Theology in America in the 19th Century.* Doctoral dissertation, Yale University, 1954.

4117   Shipley, David C. "The Development of Theology in American Methodism in the 19th Century." *London Quarterly & Holborn Review* 184 (1959): 249-264.

4118   ———. *Methodist Arminianism in the Theology of John Fletcher.* Doctoral dissertation, Yale University, 1942.

4119   Stoeffler, F. Ernest. "Pietism, the Wesleys, and Methodist Beginnings in America." In his *Continental Pietism and Early American Christianity.* Grand Rapids, MI: Wm. B. Eerdmans, 1976, 184-221.

## 6. Theological Education

4120   Brash, William Bardlsey. *The Story of Our [Theological] Colleges, 1835-1935: A Centenary Record of Ministerial Training in the Methodist Church.* London: Epworth Press, 1935. England only.

4121   Cherry, Conrad. *Hurrying toward Zion: Universities, Divinity Schools, and American Protestantism.* Bloomington: Indiana University Press, 1995.

4122    Cole, Charles E., ed. *Something More Than Human: Leaders in American Methodist Higher Education*. Nashville: General Board of Higher Education and Ministry, UMC, 1986.

4123    Fisher, Neal F. ed. *Truth and Tradition: A Conversation about the Future of United Methodist Theological Education*. Nashville : Abingdon Press, 1996.

4124    McCulloh, Gerald O. *Ministerial Education in the American Methodist Movement*. Nashville: General Board of Higher Education and Ministry, UMC, 1980.

4125    Messer, Donald E. *Calling Church and Seminary into the 21st Century*. Nashville: Abingdon Press, 1995.

4126    Miller, Glenn T. *Piety and Intellect: The Aims and Purpose of Ante-Bellum Theological Education*. Atlanta: Scholars Press, 1990.

4127    Oden, Thomas C. *Requiem: A Lament in Three Movements*. Nashville: Abingdon Press, 1995.

4128    Patterson, L. Dale. *The Ministerial Mind of American Methodism: The Courses of Study for the Ministry of the Methodist Episcopal Church, the Methodist Episcopal Church, South, and the Methodist Protestant Church, 1848-1920*. Doctoral dissertation, Drew University, 1984.

4129    Richey, Russell E. "Ministerial Education: The Early Methodist Experience," In *Theological Education in the Evangelical Tradition*, edited by D.G. Hart and R. Albert Mohler, Jr. Grand Rapids, MI: Baker Books, 1997, 45-62.

4130    Wesley, John. "Address to the Clergy" (1756). In *The Works of John Wesley*, edited by Thomas Jackson, 10:480-500.

## A. Seminary Histories

*Asbury Theological Seminary,* Wilmore, Kentucky
4131    Dayton, Donald W. *A History of Asbury Theological Seminary*. Grand Rapids: Eerdmans, 1998. Forthcoming.


*Boston University School of Theology,* Boston, Massachusetts
4132    Cameron, Richard M. *Boston University School of Theology 1839-1968*. Boston: Boston University School of Theology, 1968. *Nexus* 11/2-3, 1968.


*Candler School of Theology, Emory University,* Atlanta, Georgia
4133    Bowen, Boone M. *Candler School of Theology: Sixty Years of Service*. Atlanta: Candler School of Theology, Emory University, 1974.

**Drew University Theological School**, Madison, New Jersey

4134    Cunningham, John T. *University in the Forest: The Story of Drew University*. Florham Park, NJ: Afton Publishing Co., 1990.

4135    Richey, Russell E. "Drew Theological Seminary and American Methodism: Some Reflections." In *Scholarship, Sacraments, and Service, Historical Studies in the Protestant Tradition: Essays in Honor of Bard Thompson*, edited by Daniel B. Clendenin and W. David Buschart, 89-104. Lewiston, NY: Edwin Mellen Press, 1990.


**Duke Divinity School**, Durham, North Carolina

4136    Cushman, Robert E. "Fifty Years of Theology and Theological Education at Duke." *Duke Divinity School Review* 42/1 (Winter 1977): 3-22.

4137    Durden, Robert Franklin. *The Launching of Duke University, 1924-1949*. Durham, NC: Duke University Press, 1993


**Gammon Theological Seminary, Interdenominational Theological Center,** Atlanta, Georgia

4138    Richardson, Harry V. *Walk Together, Children: The Story of the Birth and Growth of the Interdenominational Theological Center*. Atlanta: ITC Press, 1981.


**Garrett-Evangelical Theological Seminary**, Evanston, Illinois

4139    Eller, Paul H. *Evangelical Theological Seminary, 1873-1973, Shaping Ministry*. Naperville, IL: Evangelical Theological Seminary, 1973.

4140    Norwood, Frederick A. *Dawn to Midday at Garrett*. Evanston, IL: Garrett-Evangelical Theological Seminary, 1978.


**Iliff School of Theology**, Denver, Colorado

4141    Templin, J. Alton, ed. *An Intellectual History of the Iliff School of Theology, A Centennial Tribute, 1892-1992*. Denver: Iliff School of Theology, 1992.


**Perkins School of Theology, Southern Methodist University,** Dallas, Texas

4142    Grimes, Lewis Howard. *A History of the Perkins School of Theology*. Edited by Roger Loyd. Dallas: Southern Methodist University Press, 1993.


**Theologisches Seminar der Evangelisch-Methodistischen Kirche**, Reutlingen, Germany

4143    Klaiber, Walter and Michel Weyer, eds. *Festschrift 125 Jahre Theologisches Seminar der Evangelisch-Methodistischen Kirche, 1858-1983*. Reutlingen: Theologisches Seminar der Evangelisch-Methodistischen Kirche, 1983.

**United Theological Seminary,** Dayton, Ohio

4144   *United Theological Seminary Centennial Celebration: A Collection of Essays. United Theological Seminary Bulletin* 72/1 (January 1973). Dayton, OH: Union Theological Seminary, 1973.

**Vanderbilt Divinity School,** Nashville, Tennessee

4145   Conkin, Paul K. *Gone with the Ivy: A Biography of Vanderbilt University.* Knoxville, TN: University of Tennessee Press, 1985.

4146   Thompson, Bard. *Vanderbilt Divinity School: A History.* Nashville: Vanderbilt University, 1960.

**Wesley Theological Seminary,** Washington, D.C.

4147   Chandler, Douglas R. *Pilgrimage of Faith: A Centennial History of Wesley Theological Seminary, 1882-1982.* Edited by C. C. Goen. Cabin John, MD: Seven Locks Press, 1984.


## 7. Church


### A. Historical/Theological Studies

4148   Kirkpatrick, Dow, ed. *The Doctrine of the Church.* Nashville: Abingdon Press, 1964.

4149   Methodist Church (Great Britain). *Called to Love and Praise.* Peterborough: Methodist Publishing House, 1995. 1995 Conference statement on the nature on the church.

4150   ———. *Statements of the Methodist Church on Faith and Order, 1933-1983.* Peterborough: Methodist Publishing House, 1984.

4151   Snyder, Howard A. *Models of the Kingdom.* Nashville: Abingdon Press, 1991.

4152   ———. *The Radical Wesley and Patterns for Church Renewal.* Downers Grove, IL: Inter-Varsity Press, 1980.

4153   ———. *Signs of the Spirit: How God Reshapes the Church.* Grand Rapids, MI: Academie Books, 1989.


### B. Basic Wesley Texts

*Sermons*

4154   "Of the Church" (1785). Sermon 74 in *The Works of John Wesley, Bicentennial Edition,* 3:45-57.

4155   "On Schism" (1786). Sermon 75 in *The Works of John Wesley, Bicentennial Edition,* 3:58-69.

4156 "Catholic Spirit" (1750). Sermon 39 in *The Works of John Wesley, Bicentennial Edition*, 2:79-95.

4157 "On Laying the Foundation of the New Chapel, near the City Road, London" (1777). Sermon 112 in *The Works of John Wesley, Bicentennial Edition*, 3:557-592.

4158 "On Attending the Church Service" (1787). Sermon 104 in *The Works of John Wesley, Bicentennial Edition*, 3:464-478.

*Tracts and Treatises*

4159 *The Methodist Societies: History, Nature and Design.* Edited by Rupert E. Davies. *The Works of John Wesley, Bicentennial Edition*, Vol. 9 (1989).

*Letters*

4160 "To Samuel Walker, September 24, 1755." In *The Works of John Wesley, Bicentennial Edition*, 26:592-596. Also in *John Wesley*, edited by Albert C. Outler, 73-76; see 4050.

4161 "To The Earl of Dartmouth, April 10, 1761." In *The Letters of John Wesley*, edited by John Telford, 4:146-152.

4162 "To Charles Wesley, August 18, 1785." In *The Letters of John Wesley*, edited by John Telford, 7:284-285.

4163 "To James Clark, July 3, 1756." In *The Letters of John Wesley*, edited by John Telford, 3:180-183.

## 8. The Ministry of All Christians
*See also Part IV, Section 14: Baptism.*

4164 "The Ministry of All Christians." *The Book of Discipline 1996*, par. 401-434.

4165 Carder, Kenneth L. *Living Our Beliefs: The United Methodist Way.* Nashville: Discipleship Resources, 1996.

4166 Chilcote, Paul W. *Wesley Speaks on Christian Vocation.* Nashville: Discipleship Resources, 1988.

4167 Edwards, Maldwyn. *Laymen and Methodist Beginnings Throughout the World.* Nashville: Methodist Evangelistic Materials, 1963.

4168 Koehler, George E. *The United Methodist Member's Handbook.* Revised and expanded edition. Nashville: Discipleship Resources, 1997. Leader's guide, members handbook, and filmstrip.

4169 Harkness, Georgia. *The Church and Its Laity.* Nashville: Abingdon Press, 1962.

4170   Norwood, Frederick A. *Church Membership in the Methodist Tradition.* Nashville: Abingdon Press, 1958.

4171   Rowe, Kenneth E. "Members." In *The Methodists.* By James E. Kirby, Russell E. Richey and Kenneth E. Rowe. Westport, CT: Greenwood Press, 1996, Part III, 165-254.

4172   Thurston, Branston L. *The United Methodist Way.* Revised and expanded edition. Nashville: Discipleship Resources, 1997. For new and prospective church members, or in church membership training classes.

## 9. The Ministry of Lay/Local Preachers

4173   Bowmer, John C. "The Local Preacher in Early Methodism." In *The Preacher's Handbook*, edited by David N. Francis. London: Epworth Press, 1963, 1-14.

4174   Milburn, Geoffrey and Margaret Batty, eds. *Workaday Preachers: The Story of Methodist Local Preaching.* Peterborough: Methodist Publishing House, 1995.

## 10. The Ministry of Deacons
*For works on Deaconesses, see Part III, Section 33: Women, Subsection C, North America*

4175   "The Ordained Ministry: Deacons." *The Book of Discipline 1996*, par. 319-322.

4176   Moore, Mary Elizabeth, Rosemary Skinner Keller and Gerald F. Moede. *The Diaconate in The United Methodist Tradition.* Nashville: Division of Diaconal Ministries, General Board of Higher Education and Ministry, UMC, 1986.

## 11. The Ministry of Elders

### A. Basic Statements and Current Handbooks

4177   "The Ordained Ministry: Elders." *The Book of Discipline*, 1996, par. 323-336.

4178   UMC Council of Bishops. "The Study of the Ministry of The United Methodist Church: A Report to the 1996 General Conference," *Daily Christian Advocate*, 1996, I:969-981.

4179   Campbell, Dennis M. *Who Will Go For Us? An Invitation to Ordained Ministry.* Nashville: Abingdon Press, 1994.

4180    Hunt, Richard, et al. *The Christian as Minister*. 4th edition. Nashville: Division of Ordained Ministry, Board of Higher Education and Ministry, UMC, 1997. Examines the meaning of servant ministry and leadership and outlines the steps into ordained ministry.

4181    Kohler, Robert F. *The Ministry Inquiry Process*. Nashville: Division of Ordained Ministry, General Board of Higher Education and Ministry, UMC, 1997. Workbook for persons exploring their call to ordained ministry.

4182    UMC General Board of Higher Education and Ministry. *Handbook of the Division of Ordained Ministry*. Nashville: GBHEM, Division of Ordained Ministry, 1997. Published once each quadrennium.


## B. Historical Studies

4183    Bowmer, John C. *Pastor and People: A Study of Church and Ministry in Wesleyan Methodism*. London: Epworth Press, 1975.

4184    Dunlap, E. Dale. "The United Methodist System of Itinerant Ministry." Reprinted in *Perspectives on American Methodism*, chapter 28, 415-430; see 3070.

4185    Grabner, John D. *A Commentary on the Rites of An Ordinal, The United Methodist Church [1980]*. Doctoral dissertation, University of Notre Dame, 1985; Ann Arbor, MI: University Microfilms International, 1985. See Part I, "Episcopal Methodist Ordinal Revision, 1784-1964," 1-158.

4186    Heitzenrater, Richard P. "A Critical Analysis of the Ministry Studies Since 1944." In *Perspectives on American Methodism*, chapter 29, 431-447; see 3070.

4187    Holifield, E. Brooks. *A History of Pastoral Care in America: From Salvation to Self-Realization*. Nashville: Abingdon Press, 1983.

4188    McCulloh, Gerald O., ed. *The Ministry in the Methodist Heritage*. Nashville: Department of Ministerial Education, Board of Education, The Methodist Church, 1960.

4189    Mickle, Jeffrey P. "A Comparison of the Doctrines of Ministry of Francis Asbury and Philip William Otterbein." *Perspectives on American Methodism*, chapter 6, 93-107; see 3070.

4190    Norwood, Frederick A. "The Shaping of Methodist Ministry." *Religion in Life* 43 (Autumn 1974): 337-351.

4191    Outler, Albert C. "The Ordinal." In *Companion to the Book of Worship (1966)*, Nashville: Abingdon Press, 1970, 103-144.

4192    ———. "Pastoral Care in the Wesleyan Spirit." In *The Wesleyan Theological Heritage: Essays of Albert C. Outler*, edited by Leicester R.

Longden and Thomas C. Oden, 175- 88. Grand Rapids, MI: Francis Asbury Press of Zondervan Publishing House, 1991.

4193 Steinmetz, David C. "Asbury's Doctrine of Ministry." In his *Memory and Mission, Theological Reflections on the Christian Past*. Nashville: Abingdon Press, 1988, 82-95.

## C. Theological Studies

4194 Campbell, Dennis M. *The Yoke of Obedience: The Meaning of Ordination in Methodism*. Revised edition. Nashville: Abingdon Press, 1997.

4195 Messer, Donald E. *Contemporary Images of Christian Ministry*. Nashville: Abingdon Press, 1989.

4196 ———, ed. *Send Me? The Itineracy in Crisis*. Nashville: Abingdon Press, 1991. From their respective perspectives laypersons, clergy spouses, clergy couples, and bishops explore the issues connected with itineracy, e.g. guaranteed appointments, freedom of the pulpit, open itineracy, etc.

4197 Oden, Thomas C. *Ministry through Word and Sacrament*. New York: Crossroad, 1988.

4198 ———. *Pastoral Theology: Essentials of Ministry*. San Francisco: Harper & Row, 1983.

## D. Basic Wesley Texts

*Sermons*

4199 "On Obedience to Pastors" (1785). Sermon 97 in *The Works of John Wesley, Bicentennial Edition*, 3:373-383.

4200 "On the Death of John Fletcher" (1785). Sermon 114 in *The Works of John Wesley, Bicentennial Edition*, 3:610-629.

4201 "On Visiting the Sick" (1786). Sermon 98 in *The Works of John Wesley, Bicentennial Edition*, 3:387-397.

4202 "Prophets and Priests" ["The Ministerial Office"] (1789). Sermon 121 in *The Works of John Wesley, Bicentennial Edition*, 4:72-84.

*Letters*

4203 "To James Hervey, March 20, 1739." In *The Works of John Wesley, Bicentennial Edition*, 24:609-610. Also in *John Wesley*, edited by Albert C. Outler, 70-73; see 4050.

4204 "To Samuel Walker, September 24, 1755." In *The Works of John Wesley, Bicentennial Edition*, 25:592-596. Also in *John Wesley*, edited by Albert C. Outler, 73-76; see 4050.

4205 "To Thomas Adam, October 31, 1755." In *The Works of John Wesley, Bicentennial Edition*, 25:609-611.

4218    Moede, Gerald F. *The Office of Bishop in Methodism: Its History and Development*. New York: Abingdon Press, 1964.

4219    Nelson, John R. "Methodism and the Papacy." In *A Pope for All Christians*, edited by Peter J. McCord. New York: Paulist Press, 1975, 148-175.

4220    *Position Papers and Documents, Council of Bishops, The Methodist Church 1965-1968, The United Methodist Church 1968-1984: A Bibliography.* Louisville, KY: Office of the Secretary of The Council of Bishops, UMC, 1986.

4221    Short, Roy H. *The Episcopal Leadership Role in United Methodism*. Nashville: Abingdon Press, 1985.

4222    ———. *History of The Council of Bishops of The United Methodist Church, 1939-1979*. Nashville: Abingdon Press, 1980.


### 13. Sacraments (General Studies)

4223    Borgen, Ole E. *John Wesley on the Sacraments: A Theological Study*. Nashville: Parthenon Press, 1996. Reprint of the 1973 edition.

4224    Hickman, Hoyt C. *Workbook on Communion and Baptism*. Nashville: Discipleship Resources, 1990.

4225    Knight, Henry H., III. *The Presence of God in the Christian Life: John Wesley and the Means of Grace*. Metuchen, NJ: Scarecrow Press, 1992.

4226    Sanders, Paul S. *An Appraisal of John Wesley's Sacramentalism in the Evolution of Early American Methodism*. Doctoral dissertation, Union Theological Seminary, New York, 1954.

4227    ———. "The Sacraments in Early American Methodism." *Church History* 26 (1957): 355- 371. Reprinted in *Perspectives on American Methodism*, chapter 5, 77-92.

4228    Staples, Rob L. *Outward Sign and Inward Grace: The Place of Sacraments in Wesleyan Spirituality*. Kansas City: Beacon Hill Press, 1991.

4229    Wesley, John. "The Means of Grace" (1746). Sermon 16 in *The Works of John Wesley, Bicentennial Edition*, 1:376-397.

4230    White, James F. *Sacraments as God's Self-Giving*. Nashville: Abingdon Press, 1983.


### 14. Baptism

4231    *By Water and the Spirit: A United Methodist Understanding of Baptism.* Nashville: General Board of Discipleship, 1996. Text of statement adopted by General Conference 1996; also in *Book of Resolutions* 1996.

4232  Benedict, Daniel T., Jr. *Come to the Waters: Baptism and Our Ministry of Welcoming Seekers and Making Disciples.* Nashville: Discipleship Resources, 1996.

4233  Borgen, Ole E. "Baptism, Confirmation, and Church Membership in the Methodist Church before the Union of 1968: A Historical and Theological Study." *Methodist History* 27 (1989): 89-109, 163-181.

4234  Cushman, Robert E. "Baptism and the Family of God." In *The Doctrine of the Church*, edited by Dow Kirkpatrick. Nashville: Abingdon Press, 1970.

4235  Felton, Gayle Carlton. *By Water and the Spirit: Making Connections for Identity and Ministry.* Nashville: Discipleship Resources, 1997. A resource for pastors and teachers, with commentary and full text of *By Water and the Spirit.*

4236  ———. *This Gift of Water: The Theology and Practice of Baptism among Methodists in America.* Nashville: Abingdon Press, 1993. The basic historical work.

4237  *Follow Me: Leader's Kit.* Nashville: Cokesbury Division, United Methodist Publishing House, 1989. Official confirmation resource for United Methodists. Includes handbook for pastors, parents, and congregation; student magazine; teaching plans; leader helps audiocassette; and class video.

4238  "Good News." *We Believe: Confirmation and Membership Studies for United Methodists.* Wilmore, KY: Bristol Books, 1989. Junior High and Senior High/Adult editions plus teacher's guide.

4239  Hohenstein, Charles. *The Revisions of the Rites of Baptism in the Methodist Episcopal Church, 1784-1939.* Doctoral dissertation, University of Notre Dame, 1990.

4240  Holland, Bernard. *Baptism in Early Methodism.* London: Epworth Press, 1970.

4241  Knight, Henry H., III. "The Significance of Baptism for the Christian Life: Wesley's Pattern of Christian Initiation." *Worship* 63/2 (March 1989): 133-142.

4242  "Lutheran-United Methodist Papers on Baptism." *Perkins Journal* 34 (Winter 1981): 1-56.

4243  "A Lutheran-United Methodist Statement on Baptism." *Quarterly Review* 1 (Fall 1980): 59-68. See also Lutheran and Methodist comment, 69-79. Statement and brief study guide available from Service Center, General Board of Global Ministries, UMC, Cincinnati, OH.

4244  McDonald, William P. *Gracious Voices: Shouts and Whispers for God Seekers.* Nashville: Discipleship Resources, 1997.

4245  Mutti, Fritz. *Faithful Members: The Doctrines and Duties of the Christian*

*Faith.* Nashville: Graded Press, 1988. Resource for those entering the UMC by profession of faith or from other denominations. Student book and teacher guide.

4246 Naglee, David I. *From Font to Faith: John Wesley on Infant Baptism and the Nurture of Children.* New York: Peter Lang, 1987.

4247 Neinast, Helen R. and Sidney D. Fowler. *Journey into Faith: A Confirmation Resource for Junior Highs.* Nashville: Graded Press, 1984. Pastor's guide, student book, and media kit.

4248 Ruth, Lester. *Accompanying the Journey: A Handbook for Sponsors.* Nashvile: Discipleship Resources, 1997.

4249 Stookey, Laurence H. *Baptism: Christ's Act in the Church.* Nashville: Abingdon Press, 1982. The basic theological work.

4250 Wesley, John. "The Marks of the New Birth" (1748) Sermon 18 in *The Works of John Wesley, Bicentennial Edition,* 1:415-430.

4251 ———. "The Great Privilege of Those That Are Born of God" (1748). Sermon 19 in *The Works of John Wesley, Bicentennial Edition,* 1:431-443.

4252 ———. "The New Birth" (1760). Sermon 45 in *The Works of John Wesley, Bicentennial Edition,* 2:186-201.

4253 ———. "Serious Thoughts Concerning Godfathers and Godmothers" (1752). In *The Works of John Wesley,* edited by Thomas Jackson, 10:506-509.

4254 ———. "Treatise on Baptism" (1758). In *The Works of John Wesley,* edited by Thomas Jackson, 10:188-201. Also in *John Wesley,* edited by Albert C. Outler, 318-332; see 4050.

4255 Willimon, William H. *Remember Who You Are: Baptism, a Model for Christian Life.* Nashville: The Upper Room, 1980.

## 15. Lord's Supper

4256 Bowmer, John C. *The Sacrament of the Lord's Supper in Early Methodism.* Nashville: Parthenon Press, 1996. Reprint of the 1951 edition. A classic.

4257 Cocksworth, Christopher J. *Evangelical Eucharistic Thought in the Church of England.* Cambridge: Cambridge University Press, 1993. Includes large section on John Wesley.

4258 Elliott, Daryl M. "The Lord's Supper and the United Brethren in Christ." *Methodist History* 27/4 (July 1989): 211-229.

4259 Kriewald, Diedra and Barbara P. Garcia. *Communion Book for Children.* Nashville: Discipleship Resources, 1984. Available in Spanish and English.

4260    Rattenbury, John E. *The Eucharistic Hymns of John and Charles Wesley.* Cleveland, OH: OSL Publications, 1990). A reprint of Rattenbury's 1948 edition rewritten in inclusive language. The *Hymns on the Lord's Supper*, an important appendix, remains untouched.

4261    Ruth, Lester W. "A Reconsideration of the Frequency of the Eucharist in Early American Methodism." *Methodist History* 34/1 (October 1995): 47-58.

4262    Sanders, Paul S. "Wesley's Eucharistic Faith and Practice." *Anglican Theological Review* 148 (February 1966): 154-174. Reprinted in *Doxology* 5 (1988): 21-34.

4263    Stookey, Laurence H. *Eucharist: Christ's Feast with the Church.* Nashville: Abingdon Press, 1993.

4264    Wainwright, Geoffrey. *Eucharist and Eschatology.* New York: Oxford University Press, 1982. Reprint of 1971 edition.

4265    Wesley, John. "The Duty of Constant Communion" (1732, reissued 1787). Sermon 101 in *The Works of John Wesley, Bicentennial Edition*, 3:427-439. Also in *John Wesley*, edited by Albert C. Outler, 332-344; see 4050.

4266    ———, and Charles Wesley. *Hymns on the Lord's Supper.* Madison, NJ: Charles Wesley Society, 1995. Facsimile reprint of first, 1745 edition. One hundred sixty-six hymns plus a digest of Brevint's *Christian Sacrament and Sacrifice* (1673), with judicious introduction by Geoffrey Wainwright.

4267    Willimon, William H. *Sunday Dinner: The Lord's Supper and the Christian Life.* Nashville: The Upper Room, 1981.

## 16. Theological Ethics
*See also Part III, Section 31: Social Thought and Action.*

4268    Beach, Waldo and H. Richard Niebuhr, eds. *Christian Ethics.* New York: Roland Press, 1955. See "John Wesley," 353-365.

4269    Birch, Bruce C. and Larry L. Rasmussen. *Bible and Ethics in the Christian Life.* Revised and expanded edition. Minneapolis: Augsburg, 1989.

4270    Eli, R. George. *Social Holiness: John Wesley's Thinking on Christian Community and Its Relationship to the Social Order.* New York: Peter Lang, 1993.

4271    Gustafson, James. *Christ and the Moral Life.* Chicago: University of Chicago Press, 1968.

4272    Hauerwas, Stanley. *After Christendom: How the Church Is to Behave if*

*Freedom, Justice, and a Christian Nation Are Bad Ideas.* Nashville: Abingdon Press, 1991.

4273 ———. *Character and the Christian Life: A Study in Theological Ethics.* San Antonio, TX: Trinity University Press, 1975.

4274 ———. "Christianizing Perfection: Second Thoughts on Character and Sanctification." In *Wesleyan Theology Today*, edited by Theodore H. Runyon, 251-263; see 4016.

4275 ——— and William H. Willimon. *Resident Aliens: Life in the Christian Colony.* Nashville: Abingdon Press, 1989.

4276 Hulley, Leonard D. *To Be and to Do: Exploring Wesley's Thought on Ethical Behaviour.* Pretoria: University of South Africa, 1988.

4277 Hynson, Leon T. *To Reform the Nation: The Theological Foundations of Wesley's Ethics.* Grand Rapids, MI: Francis Asbury Press of Zondervan Publishing House, 1985.

4278 Jennings, Theodore W., Jr. *Good News to the Poor: John Wesley's Evangelical Economics.* Nashville: Abingdon Press, 1990.

4279 Jones, Major J. *Christian Ethics for Black Theology.* Nashville: Abingdon Press, 1974.

4280 Marquardt, Manfred. *John Wesley's Social Ethics: Praxis and Principles.* Nashville: Abingdon Press, 1992.

4281 Meeks, M. Douglas. *God the Economist: The Doctrine of God and Political Economy.* Minneapolis: Fortress Press, 1989.

4282 Ogletree, Thomas W. *The Use of the Bible in Christian Ethics: A Constructive Essay.* Philadelphia: Fortress Press, 1983.

4283 *Poverty and Ecclesiology: Nineteenth-Century Evangelicals in the Light of Liberation Theology. Edited by Justo González, et al.* Collegeville, MN: Liturgical Press, 1992.

4284 Seifert, Harvey. *What on Earth? Making Personal Decisions on Controversial Issues.* Nashville: Discipleship Resources for Church and Society, 1991.

4285 Wogaman, J. Philip. *Christian Moral Judgment.* Philadelphia: Westminster Press, 1989.

4286 ———. *Making Moral Decisions.* Nashville: Abingdon Press, 1990.

# PART V: POLITY

*For publicagtions issued after December 1997, consult UM Studies: Basic Bibliographies at www.gcah.org.*

## 1. Basic Texts: United Methodist Church

5001     *The Book of Discipline of The United Methodist Church, 1996.* Nashville: United Methodist Publishing House, 1996. Available in English, Korean, and Spanish.

5002     *The Book of Resolutions of The United Methodist Church, 1996.* Nashville: United Methodist Publishing House, 1997. Software edition of *Book of Discipline* and *Book of Resolutions* available in Windows and Macintosh versions. *Book of Resolutions* not available separately. Available from Cokesbury.

5003     *The Decisions of the Judicial Council, 1968-1992.* Nashville: United Methodist Publishing House, 1989-1993. 2 vols. For decisions 1993 and following, see appendix to the *General Minutes*, published annually. Software edition *Judicial Council Decisions of the UMC 1940-1996* available in Windows and Macintosh versions. Available from Cokesbury.

5004     *Guidelines for Leading Your Congregation, 1997-2000.* Nashville: Abingdon Press, 1996. Thirty booklets developed by the Interagency Task Force on resources to provide guidance for the program and administration of the congregation.

5005     Hawkins, Thomas. *Job Descriptions & Leadership Training for Local Church Leaders, 1997-2000.* Nashville: Discipleship Resources, 1997. Thirty-eight leaflets for each of the major tasks and responsibilities in the church council, plus study guide *Training Church Leaders and Using Job Descriptions.*

5006     *Manual on Shared Facilities.* Edited by James A Craig. New York: General Board of Global Ministries, UMC, 1996.

## 2. Basic Texts: Methodist Church (Great Britain)

5007   *Constitutional Practice and Discipline of the Methodist Church.* Peterborough: Methodist Publishing House, 1988. Vol. 1: Historical documents amended by act of Parliament only, first published in 1951, 7th edition, 1988. Vol. 2: Standing orders, updated annually.

## 3. Current Handbooks

5008   Tuell, Jack M. *The Organization of The United Methodist Church.* Revised 1997-2000 edition. Nashville: Abingdon Press, 1997.

5009   Jones, Ezra Earl. *Think about It: Reflections on Quality and The United Methodist Church.* Nashville: Discipleship Resources, 1995.

## 4. History and Development

5010   Baker, Frank. "Polity." In *A History of the Methodist Church in Great Britain,* edited by Rupert E. Davies & Gordon Rupp, 1:211-256; see 3010.

5011   Behney, J. Bruce and Paul H. Eller. *The History of the Evangelical United Brethren Church.* Nashville: Abingdon Press, 1979. Check index.

5012   Buckley, James M. *Constitutional and Parliamentary History of the Methodist Episcopal Church.* New York: Eaton & Mains, 1912.

5013   Campbell, Dennis, ed. "United Methodism & American Culture: Direction, Discipline, Diversity, Doctrine." *Circuit Rider* [special issue] 20/9 (November 1996): 1-34.

5014   Curts, Lewis, ed. *The General Conferences of the Methodist Episcopal Church from 1792-1896.* Cincinnati: Curts & Jennings; New York: Eaton & Mains, 1900. Useful outline history of general conferences of the MEC through 1896.

5015   Davies, Rupert E. "Introduction" to *The Works of John Wesley, Bicentennial Edition.* Vol. 9: *The Methodist Societies, I: History, Nature, and Design*; see 4041.

5016   Drinkhouse, Edward J. *History of Methodist Reform, Synoptical of General Methodism 1703-1789, with Special and Comprehensive Reference to Its Most Salient Exhibition in the History of the Methodist Protestant Church.* 2 vols. Baltimore: Board of Publication of the Methodist Protestant Church, 1899.

5017   Drury, Augustus W., ed. *The Disciplines of the United Brethren in Christ, 1814-1841.* Nashville: Parthenon Press, 1996. Reprint of the 1895 edition.

5018   ———, ed. *Minutes of the Annual and General Conferences of the Church of the United Brethren in Christ, 1900-1818.* Nashville: Parthenon Press, 1996. Reprint of the 1897 edition.

5019    Evangelical Association. *Glaubenslehre und Allgemeine Regeln Chritslicher Kirchenzucht und Ordnung der sogenannten Albrechts-Leute.* Nashville: Parthenon Press, 1996. Reprint of the 1809 EV discipline.

5020    ———. *Glaubenslehre und Kirchen-Zucht-Ordnung der Evangelische Gemeinschaft.* Zweite und verbesserte Auflage. Nashville: Parthenon Press, 1996. Reprint of the 1817 EV discipline.

5021    Frank, Thomas E. *Polity, Practice, and The Mission of the United Methodist Church.* Nashville: Abingdon Press, 1997. The basic work.

5022    Harmon, Nolan B. *The Organization of the Methodist Church.* 2nd revised edition. Nashville: United Methodist Publishing House, 1962. Originally published in 1948, this twice-revised book is the standard work on the history and development of Methodist polity.

5023    King, William M. "Denominational Modernization and Religious Identity: The Case of the Methodist Episcopal Church." *Methodist History* 20/2 (January 1982): 75-89. Reprinted in *Perspectives on American Methodism*, chapter 23, 343-355; see 3070.

5024    Kirby, James E., Russell E. Richey and Kenneth E. Rowe. *The Methodists.* Westport, CT: Greenwood Press, 1996.

5025    Methodist Episcopal Church. *Minutes of the Annual Conferences of the Methodist Episcopal Church for the Years 1773-1828.* Nashville: Parthenon Press, 1996. Reprint of the 1840 edition.

5026    *Methodist General Rules and Disciplines.* Library of Methodist Classics. Nashville: United Methodist Publishing House, 1992. Facsimile reprints of Wesley's 1743 *General Rules*, along with the first five books of discipline of the Methodist Episcopal Church, 1785-1789.

5027    Nickerson, Michael G. *Sermons, Systems, and Strategies: the Geographic Strategies of the Methodist Episcopal Church in its Expansion into New York State, 1788-1810.* Doctoral dissertation, Syracuse University, 1988.

5028    Norwood, Frederick A., ed. *The Methodist Discipline of 1789, including the Annotations of Thomas Coke and Francis Asbury.* Nashville: Parthenon Press, 1996. Reprint of the 1979 edition. Facsimile reprint of the 1798 *Discipline* with notes and commentary by the church's first two bishops.

5029    Perry, Stephen. "The Revival of Stewardship and the Creation of the World Service Commission in the Methodist Episcopal Church, 1912-1924." *Methodist History* 23/1 (July 1985): 223-239. Reprinted in *Perspectives on American Methodism*, chapter 27, 400-414; see 3070.

5030    Peterson, Peter A. *History of the Revisions of the Discipline of the*

*Methodist Episcopal Church, South*. Nashville: Publishing House of the Methodist Episcopal Church, South, 1889.

5031    Primer, Ben. *Protestants and American Business Methods*. Ann Arbor, MI: UMI Research Press, 1979.

5032    Richey, Russell E. *The Methodist Conference in America: A History*. Nashville: Kingswood Books, 1996.

5033    Sherman, David. *History of the Revisions of the Discipline of the Methodist Episcopal Church*. New York: Hunt & Eaton, 1880.

5034    Stevens, Abel. *An Essay on Church Polity: Comprehending an Outline of the Controversy on Ecclesiastical Government, and a Vindication of the Ecclesiastical System of the Methodist Episcopal Church*. New York: Lane & Tippett for the MEC, 1845. Ten revised editions through 1870.

5035    Tigert, John J. *Constitutional History of American Episcopal Methodism*. 6th edition, revised and enlarged. Nashville: Parthenon Press, 1996. Reprint of the 1916 edition.

5036    Trachtenberg, Alan. *The Incorporation of America: Culture and Society in the Gilded Age*. New York: Hill and Wang, 1982.

5037    Wansbrough, Charles E. *Handbook and Index to the Minutes of the Conference showing the Growth and Development of the Wesleyan Methodist Constitution from the first Conference, 1744 to 1890*. London: Wesleyan Methodist Book Room, 1890.

5038    Wesley, John. "Minutes of the Conference 1744-1747." In *John Wesley*, edited by Albert C. Outler, 134-181; see 4050.

5039    ———. "The Nature, Design and General Rules of the United Societies" (1743). In *The Works of John Wesley, Bicentennial Edition*, 9:67-79. Cf. *The Book of Discipline*, 1996, Part III, 66-69.

5040    ———. "A Plain Account of the People called Methodists" (1749). In *The Works of John Wesley, Bicentennial Edition*, 9:253-280.

# PART VI: PERIODICALS

*For revisions and additions to this list of periodicals, including a list of Methodist periodicals by country from Angola to Zimbabwe, consult UM Studies: Basic Bibliographies at www.gcah.org.*

## 1. Bibliographies

6001 *A Checklist of British Methodist Periodicals*. Compiled by E. Alan Rose. London: World Methodist Historical Society Publications, 1981. One hundred forty-two titles from 1778 to 1980.

6002 *Union List of United Methodist Serials, 1773-1973*. Compiled by John and Lyda Batsel. Evanston: General Commission on Archives and History, UMC, with the United Methodist Librarians' Fellowship and Garrett Theological Seminary, 1974.

## 2. Indexes

6003 *Methodist History Index, 1962-1982*. Madison, NJ: General Commission on Archives and History, UMC, 1982, 1998. Vol.1, 1962-82; vol. 2, 1982-97.

6004 *Methodist Reviews Index, 1818-1985*. Compiled by Elmer J. O'Brien. 2 vols. Nashville: General Board of Higher Education and Ministry, UMC, 1989. Vol. 1, Periodical Articles; Vol. 2, Book Reviews.

6005 *Religion Index One: Periodicals*. Chicago: American Theological Library Association, 1949–. Issues for 1949-1959 published as *Index to Religious Periodical Literature*. Also available in CD-Rom format.

6006 *The United Methodist Periodical Index*. Nashville: United Methodist Publishing House, 1961-1980. Issues for 1961-1965 published as *Methodist Periodical Index*. An important twenty-year index to official

United Methodist publications, including curriculum. No longer published.

6007  *Proceedings of the Wesley Historical Society: General Index to Vols. 1-30 and Publications 1-4, 1897-1956.* Compiled by John A. Vickers. London: Wesley Historical Society, 1960; *General Index to Vols. 31-50 (1957-1996).* London: The Society, 1997.

## 3. The Current Basics

6008  *Christian Social Action.* Published monthly by the General Board of Church and Society.

6009  *Circuit Rider.* United Methodist clergy journal published bi-monthly by The United Methodist Publishing House.

6010  *The Interpreter.* Spanish version: *El Intérprete.* Korean version: *United Methodist Family.* Monthly program journals with news supplement published by United Methodist Communications.

6011  *Methodist History.* Published quarterly by the General Commission on Archives and History, UMC.

6012  *Quarterly Review.* A scholarly journal for reflection on ministry published by The United Methodist Publishing House and the General Board of Higher Education and Ministry, UMC.

6013  *United Methodist Newscope.* A national weekly newsletter for United Methodist leaders published by The United Methodist Publishing House.

6014  *United Methodist Reporter.* An independent national weekly newspaper published by United Methodist Communications Council, Dallas, Texas.

## 4. General Agency Periodicals

General Board of Church and Society

6015  *Christian Social Action.*

6016  *Current Scene.*

6017  *DAC Bulletin: A Bulletin of Drug and Alcohol Concerns* (Department of Human Welfare).

6018  *Environmental Justice News.*

6019  *Peace with Justice Newsletter.*

6020  *Word from Washington* (Department of Field Service).

## General Board of Discipleship

6021 *Alive Now!* (The Upper Room).
6022 *El Aposento Alto* (The Upper Room).
6023 *Camp Memo* (Christian Education Section).
6024 *Church School Today* (Curriculum Resources Committee).
6025 *Covenant Discipleship Quarterly* (Section on Covenant Discipleship).
6026 *Curriculum Memo* (Curriculum Resources Committee).
6027 *Devo'zine* (The Upper Room devotional guide for youth).
6028 *Discipleship Dateline* (Office of Communication & Interpretation).
6029 *Discipleship Trends* (Office of Research).
6030 *Discípulos Responsables.*
6031 *Ethnic Minority Local Church News Network* (Mission Priority Section).
6032 *Family Ministries Networker* (Section on Ministry of the Laity).
6033 *General Board of Discipleship Dateline* (Office of Communications & Interpretation).
6034 *Hallelujah!* (Section on Worship).
6035 *Horizons: Older Adult Ministry* (Section on Ministry of the Laity).
6036 *Information: Children's Ministries* (Section on Ministry of the Laity).
6037 *Jubilate: A Newsletter for United Methodist Musicians* (Section on Worship).
6038 *Lay Witness Newsletter* (Section on Evangelism).
6039 *Life Span* (Section on Ministry of the Laity).
6040 *Links* (Section on Ministry of the Laity).
6041 *The Living Prayer Newsletter* (The Upper Room).
6042 *Logos* (Section on Evangelism).
6043 *Men and Faith.*
6044 *MensNews* (United Methodist Men).
6045 *New Congregational Development* (Section on Evangelism).
6046 *Newsletter of Persons with Handicapping Conditions* (Jointly published by The Upper Room and the Division of Health and Welfare Ministries, General Board of Global Ministries, UMC).
6047 *Notes for Lay Leaders* (Section on Ministry of the Laity).
6048 *Offering Christ Today* (Discipleship Ministries Unit).
6049 *Peace Advocate* (Section on Ministry of the Laity).
6050 *People to People* (Curriculum Resources Committee).
6051 *Plain Talk About Lay Speaking* (Section on Ministry of the Laity).
6052 *Pockets* (The Upper Room).
6053 *Singles in Service* (Section on Ministry of the Laity).
6054 *Sunday School Extension Network* (Christian Education).
6055 *Touching* (The Upper Room Aids ministry).
6056 *United Methodist News* (Korean).

6057　*United Methodist Stewardship Network Newsletter* (Section on Stewardship).

6058　*The Upper Room.*

6059　*Volunteer News* (The Upper Room).

6060　*Walk to Emmaus International Newsletter* (The Upper Room).

6061　*Weavings: A Journal of the Christian Spiritual Life* (The Upper Room).

6062　*Wings: A Newsletter on Disability, Aging, and Christian Faith* (The Upper Room).

6063　*Worship Newsletter* (Section on Worship).

6064　*Young Adult Newsletter* (Section on Ministry of the Laity).

6065　*Youth Express* (NYMO).

6066　*Youth Ministry Resource Exchange* (Section on Ministry of the Laity).

6067　*Youth Servant Team Update* (Section on Ministry of the Laity).

## General Board of Global Ministries

6068　*Awareness* (Affirmative action newsletter).

6069　*Church and Community* (National Division).

6070　*Community Developers* (National Division).

6071　*Friends in Mission* (Mission Education Cultivation Program Department).

6072　*Knock* (UM Volunteers in Mission).

6073　*Messenger* (Health & Welfare Ministries Program Department).

6074　*Mission Papers.*

6075　*Mission Stories* (Mission Education Cultivation Program Department).

6076　*New World Outlook* (Mission Education Cultivation Program Department).

6077　*News and Views* (National Division).

6078　*Newsletter of Persons with Handicapping Conditions* (Jointly published by Health and Welfare Ministries and The Upper Room, General Board of Discipleship).

6079　*Response* (United Methodist Women).

6080　*740 Plan* (General Secretary).

6081　*Short-Term Volunteers in Mission* (Mission Personnel Resources Program Department).

6082　*Turning Points* (National Division).

6083　*U. M. Congress of the Deaf* (Health and Welfare Ministries Program Department).

6084　*UMCOR Update* (United Methodist Committee on Relief).

## General Board of Higher Education and Ministry

6085　*Access* (Division of Higher Education).

6086　*Across the Boards* (Division of Ordained Ministry).

6087　*Bottom Line* (Office of Loans and Scholarships).

6088    *Cite* (Association of United Methodist Theological Schools: Committee on Global Theological Education).

6089    *Coast to Coast* (Division of Higher Education).

6090    *Colleague* (Office of Interpretation).

6091    *Diaconal Ministry Networker* (Division of Diaconal Ministry).

6092    *Ethnic Minority Clergy News* (Division of Ordained Ministry).

6093    *I. E.,* Newsletter of International Education (National Association of Schools and Colleges of The UMC).

6094    *Impact* (Division of Chaplains and Related Ministries).

6095    *Keepin' in Touch* (Division of Higher Education, Campus Ministry Section).

6096    *Lex Collegii* (Division of Higher Education).

6097    *New Perspectives* (Division of Higher Education).

6098    *New Witnesses* (Division of Ordained Ministry).

6099    *Occasional Papers* (Office of Interpretation).

6100    *On Board* (General Secretary's newsletter).

6101    *Orientation* (Campus Ministry Division).

6102    *Persons and Positions Available* (Division of Diaconal Ministry).

6103    *Presidential Papers* (Division of Higher Education).

6104    *Prism: A Quarterly Journal for Retired United Methodist Clergy and Spouses* (Jointly published with the General Board of Pensions).

6105    *Public Policy Update* (Division of Higher Education).

6106    *Quarterly Review* (with United Methodist Publishing House).

6107    *The Source* (Division of Ordained Ministry).

6108    *Update* (Division of Higher Education, Black College Fund).

6109    *Washington Newsletter* (Division of Higher Education).

6110    *Wellsprings: A Journal for United Methodist Clergywomen* (Division of Ordained Ministry).

## General Board of Pensions and Health Benefits

6111    *For Your Benefit.*

6112    *News & Views.*

6113    *Pension Updates.*

6114    *Prism: A Quarterly Journal for Retired United Methodist Clergy and Spouses* (Jointly published with the Division of Ordained Ministry, General Board of Higher Education and Ministry, UMC).

## General Commission on Archives and History

6115    *Action Memo* (newsletter).

6116    *Methodist History* (scholarly journal). Index to Vols. 1-20, 1962-82.

**General Commission on Religion and Race**
6117   *United Methodist Monitor.*

**General Commission on the Status and Role of Women**
6118   *The Flyer.*

**General Commission on United Methodist Men**
   *Men's News*
   *UM Men United*

**General Council on Finance and Administration**
6119   *Newsline* (local church insurance program newsletter).
6120   *Target* (insurance concerns).

**General Council on Ministries**
6121   *Facts and Figures* (Office of Research).
6122   *Signs of the Times* (Office of Research).
6123   *Viewpoint* (Office of Research).

**United Methodist Communications**
6124   *CW Update* (Circuit Writer Network).
6125   *Come/Share/Rejoice in Giving.*
6126   *Heads Up* (General Secretary's newsletter).
6127   *El Intérprete.*
6128   *Interpreter.*
6129   *Keeping You Posted* (Department of Public Relations).
6130   *Methodists Make News.*
6131   *Network* (United Methodist Communicators).
6132   *News/News Service of the UMC.*
6133   *Transmitter* (Division of Public Media).
6134   *TV/T Newsletter* (Television/Telecommunications Fund).
6135   *United Methodist Communicator* (Department of Public Relations).
6136   *United Methodist Family* (Korean-language program journal).

**United Methodist Publishing House**
6137   *Around the House* (Employee newsletter).
6138   *Church Library News* (Cokesbury).
6139   *Church Music Workshop.*
6140   *Church Secretary Newsletter* (Cokesbury).
6141   *Circuit Rider.*
6142   *Disciple* (Disciple Bible Study program).

6143   *Forecast* (Cokesbury). (Quarterly catalog of resources for church, Sunday-school, and fellowship groups.)
6144   *Leader in the Church Today.*
6145   *The Magazine for Youth.*
6146   *Mature Years.*
6147   *Open Circuit.*
6148   *Quarter Notes for Leaders of Music with Children.*
6149   *Quarterly Review* (Published jointly with General Board of Higher Education and Ministry).
6150   *Store Newsletter* (Cokesbury).
6151   *Teacher in the Church Today.*
6152   *Ultimo Hora* (Cokesbury).
6153   *United Methodist Newscope.*
6154   *Youth Net.*

## 5. Annual Conference and Area Periodicals
*For full list with addresses see current* United Methodist Directory.

## 6. Affiliated Group Periodicals

**Aldersgate Renewal Ministries/United Methodist Renewal Services Fellowship (Charismatic)**
6155   *Aldersgate Journal.*
6156   *ARM Ministry Update.*

**Christian Educators Fellowship**
6157   *CEF Newsline.*

**Disciplined Order of Christ**
6158   *New Life News.*

**Fellowship of United Methodists in Music and Worship Arts**
6159   *Worship Arts.*

**Foundation for Evangelism**
6160   *Forward.*
6161   *The Foundation for Evangelism.*

## Order of Saint Luke
6162   *Doxology.*
6163   *The Font* (newsletter).
6164   *Sacramental Life.*

## Professional Association of UM Church Secretaries
6165   *Vital Link.*

## United Methodist Association of Church Business Administrators
6166   *UMACBA Newsletter.*

## United Methodist Association of Health and Welfare Ministries
6167   *The UMA Journal.*

# 7. Caucus Periodicals
*Unofficial special interest/advocacy groups.*
*For addresses, see current United Methodist Directory.*

## Affirmation, United Methodists for Lesbian, Gay, and Bisexual Concerns
6168   *Affirmation Newsletter.*

## Black Methodists for Church Renewal (BMCR)
6169   *Now.*

## Bush Meeting Dutch (An association for local history and genealogy of the former Evangelical United Brethren Church, its predecessors, and sister churches)
6170   *Bush Meeting Dutch.*

## Charismatics
6171   See Aldersgate Renewal Ministries, 6155 and 6156.

## Charles Wesley Society
6172   *Charles Wesley Society Newsletter.*
6173   *Proceedings of the Charles Wesley Society.*

## Coalition of Black United Methodist Clergywomen
6174   *Womanist Wisdom.*

**Concerned Methodists**
6175   *Christian Methodist Newsletter.*

**Confessing Movement**
6176   *We Confess.*

**Connection of Evangelical Clergywomen**
6177   *The Credence Connection.*

**Ed Robb Evangelistic Association**
6178   *Challenge to Evangelism Today.*

**Florida Conference Committee on Hispanic Ministry**
6179   *Metohispano.*

**Good News**
6180   *Catalyst* (newsletter for seminarians).
6181   *Focus.*
6182   *Good News.*

**Historical Society of The United Methodist Church**
6183   *Historian's Digest.*

**Institute on Religion and Democracy (United Methodists for Faith and Freedom)**
6184   *Partnership Briefing.*
6185   *UM Action Briefing.*

**International Church Computer Users Network**
6186   *Computers in the Church.*

**MARCHA (Methodists Associated Representing the Cause of Hispanic Americans)**
6187   *MARCHA Bolitan.*

**Methodist Federation for Social Action**
6188   *Social Questions Bulletin.*

**Methodists United for Peace and Justice**
6189   *Peace Leaf.*

**Mexican American Program, Perkins School of Theology**
6190   *Apuntes.*

**Mission Society for United Methodists**
6191   *Mission Advocate.*

**National Federation of Asian American United Methodists**
6192   *Asian American News.*

**National Fellowship of Associate Members and Local Pastors of the UMC**
6193   *The Source* (newsletter).

**National Filipino American United Methodists**
6194   *Chronicle.*

**National Japanese American United Methodist Caucus**
6195   *Hono-o.*

**Native American International Caucus**
6196   *Echo of the Four Winds.*

**Physically Handicapped United Methodist Persons**
6197   *Wings.*

**Reconciling Congregation Program**
6198   *Katalyst* (newsletter).
6199   *Open Hands.*

**Renew Network (Evangelical Coalition for United Methodist Women)**
6200   *Renew.*

**Southern Asian National Caucus of United Methodists**
6201   *South Asian American News.*

**Taskforce of United Methodists on Abortion and Sexuality**
6202   *Lifewatch.*

**Transforming Congregations Program**
6203   *Transforming Congregations Newsletter.*

**United Methodist Asian Caucus**
6204   *Asian American News.*

**United Methodist Clergy Couples**
6205   *Marriage and Ministry.*

**United Methodist Fellowship of Healing**
6206   *Healing Frontiers.*

**United Methodist Renewal Services Fellowship (see Aldersgate Renewal Ministries).**

**United Methodist Rural Fellowship**
6207   *United Methodist Rural Fellowship Bulletin.*

**United Methodist Women's Caucus**
6208   *Yellow Ribbon.*

**United Methodists for Faith and Freedom (see Institute on Religion and Democracy).**

**Wesley Studies Society (Greensboro, NC)**
6209   *The Aldersgate.*

**Wesleyan Theological Society**
6210   *Wesleyan Theological Journal.*


## 8.   Theological Seminary Journals

**Asbury Theological Seminary**
6211   *Asbury Theological Journal.*
6212   *Wesleyan Holiness Studies Center Bulletin.*

**Boston University School of Theology**
6213   *Anna Howard Shaw Center Newsletter.*

**Interdenominational Theological Center (includes UMC's Gammon Theological Seminary)**
6214   *Journal of the Interdenominational Theological Center.*

**Methodist School of Theology in Ohio**
6215   *Journal of Theology* (Published jointly with United Theological Seminary).

**Theologischen Seminar der Evangelisch Methodistischen Kirche, Reutlingen, Germany**
6216   *Freundeskreis Mitteilungen.*

6217    *Theologie fur die Praxis.*

## United Theological Seminary, Dayton, OH
6218    *Telescope-Messenger* (newsletter, The Center for the Evangelical United Brethren Heritage).
6219    *Journal of Theology.* (Published jointly with Methodist School of Theology in Ohio).


## 9.  Larger Methodist Family in the United States

6220    *A.M.E. Church Review.*
6221    *A.M.E. Zion Quarterly Review.*
6222    *Arminian* (Fundamental Wesleyan Society).
6223    *Christian Index* (C.M.E. Church).
6224    *Christian Recorder* (A.M.E. Church).
6225    *Evangelical Advocate* (Evangelical Church).
6226    *Evangelical Methodist Bulletin* (Evangelical Methodist Church).
6227    *Herald of Holiness* (Church of the Nazarene).
6228    *Light and Life* (Free Methodist Church).
6229    *Methodist Protestant Councillor* (Methodist Protestant Church).
6230    *Star of Zion* (A.M.E. Zion Church).
6231    *U B Newsletter* (Church of the United Brethren in Christ).
6232    *Wesleyan Advocate* (The Wesleyan Church).


## 10.  World Methodist Family
*For addresses, consult 2013, or contact: Periodicals Supervisor, Methodist Library, Drew University Theological School, Madison, NJ 07940; phone (793) 408-3590; fax (793) 408-3909; jrubinet@drew.edu.*

6233    *Boletin de CIEMAL* (Council of Latin American Evangelical Churches).
6234    *Flame* (World Evangelism Committee of the World Methodist Council).
6235    *Historical Bulletin* (World Methodist Historical Society).
6236    *OxfordNotes* (Newsletter of the Oxford Institute of Methodist Theological Studies).
6237    *Tree of Life* (World Federation of Methodist and United Church Women).
6238    *World Parish* (World Methodist Council).

# PART VII: VIDEO RESOURCES

*The following resources are available in the standard video formats. Many are available through annual conference audio-visual lending libraries and through EcuFilm, a United Methodist sponsored ecumenical film/video distribution service. (Addresses are given in Part VIII.)*

## 1. Historical Surveys
*See also videos listed under African American Methodists, Francis Asbury, and John Wesley.*

7001    *Barratt's Chapel, Cradle of Methodism.* A visual introduction to one of The UMC's historic shrines in Frederica, near Dover, Delaware, erected in 1780. In this chapel on November 14, 1784, Wesley's emissary to America, Bishop Thomas Coke, laid out Wesley's plan for an independent church. Coke celebrated American Methodism's first Lord's Supper here during that visit. Produced for the Friends of Barratt's Chapel, 1997. 20 minutes.

7002    *Burning Bright.* Through a combination of live-action photography and historic graphics this film presents major aspects of the history of The United Methodist Church and other churches of Methodist origin in the United States. Produced by United Methodist Communications and the General Commission on Archives and History, 1975. 32 minutes.

7003    *Claiming the Story: A Journey in Christian History for United Methodists.* Privately produced for James E. Miller by Envisions, 327 East Wayne St., Suite 250, Fort Wayne, IN, 46802. 1988. 35 minutes.

7004    *From the Word Go.* This magazine-format resource gives a variety of glimpses into the history and tradition of The United Methodist Church. It also captures contemporary images of United Methodist people. Produced by United Methodist Communications, 1984. 35 minutes.

7005    *One Faith, Many Visions.* Depicts United Methodist heritage and contemporary expressions of ministry. Produced for the Bicentennial of American Methodism by Wesley Theological Seminary, Washington, DC, 1984. 30 minutes.

7006 *Politeness and Enthusiasm, 1689-1791.* In the 18th century two forms of Christianity appeared: that of the elite—with an educated, "reasonable" God—and a more active form of Christianity, which discovered God to be gracious and experienceable. Essential background for understanding the rise of Methodism. Part of *The Christians* series, produced by McGraw-Hill Book Co., 1984. 38 minutes.

7007 *Sharing the Heritage: The History of United Methodism in America.* Privately produced for James Miller by Envisions, 327 East Wayne St., Suite 250, Fort Wayne, IN, 46802. 1988. 32 minutes.

7008 *This is Methodism.* Video of the story of Methodism in Great Britain from John Wesley to the present day. Produced by the Methodist Publishing House, London, 1990.

## 2. People, Movements, and Ministries

### A. African American Methodists

*See also video on William Wilberforce, 7074.*

7009 *Black Methodism: Legacy of Faith.* Traces the history of African American United Methodists from the 18th century to the present. Narrated by Hilly Hicks, featuring Professor William B. McClain of Wesley Theological Seminary. Produced by the Advance Committee of the GCOM and UMCom, 1994. 28 minutes.

7010 *Let a New Earth Rise.* Features student interviews and highlights from the 11 historically black United States colleges and universities related to the United Methodist Church. Produced by United Methodist Communications, 1997. 20 minutes.

7011 *The Richard Allen Story.* Produced for the bicentennial of the African Methodist Episcopal Church by Studio II Productions, Philadelphia, 1987. 35 minutes.

### B. Asbury, Francis

7012 *Francis Asbury.* The story of his life and ministry. Produced by the Continuing Theological Education Department of Drew University Theological School, 1983. 25 minutes.

### C. Asian American Methodists

7013 *Picture Brides: Lives of Hawaii's Early Immigrant Women from Japan, Okinawa, and Korea.* Produced by Alice Yun Chai and Barbara

Kawakami, Hawaii University Department of Women's Studies, 1995. With study guide. 27 minutes.

## D. Candler School of Theology, Emory University

7014    *Seeing Visions, Dreaming Dreams: Celebrating Candler's 75th Anniversary.* Produced by Candler School of Theology, 1989.

## E. Class Meeting

7015    *Class Leaders Teleconference.* Videotape of the live 90-minute teleconference on class leaders broadcast in May 1991. Produced by the Covenant Discipleship and Christian Formation Section of the General Board of Discipleship, 1991. 90 minutes.

7016    *Discovering the Modern Methodists.* This two-tape, 80-minute video narrated by David Lowes Watson contains a four-part presentation on the early Methodist class meeting and modern covenant discipleship groups. Produced by the General Board of Discipleship, 1988. Part of Covenant Discipleship Congregation Kit. 80 minutes.

7017    *We Are the Branches.* Explains how branch groups work and shows the impact that the experience has on young people. Produced cooperatively by the Office of Covenant Discipleship and Christian Formation, Section on Christian Education and Age-Level Ministries, and the National Youth Ministry Organization, 1991. Available from Discipleship Resources.

## F. Consultation on Church Union

7018    *Churches in Covenant Communion.* Reviews covenant proposal between seven mainline Protestant churches. Princeton, NJ: COCU, 1990.

## G. Diaconal Ministries

*See also* The Deaconess Story *in Section Z2: Women, 7077.*

7019    *A Call to Serve.* Shows the variety of ways Diaconal ministers express their vocation and call. Produced by the Division of Diaconal Ministries, General Board of Higher Education and Ministry, 1988. 25 minutes.

7020    *Service to the World.* The story of diaconal ministry in the United Methodist Church. Produced by the Division of Diaconal Ministry, General Board of Higher Education and Ministry, 1986. 20 minutes.

## H. Disciplined Order of Christ

7021    *Disciplined Order of Christ: Celebrating 50 Years of Becoming a New Creation in Christ.* Produced for the Disciplined Order of Christ by Open Door Ministries, 1993.

## I. Ethnicity

7022    *The Charter for Racial Justice: A History.* Developed by The Council on Interracial Books for Children, Inc. for the Women's Division, GBGM, UMC, 1983. Includes study/action guide and racial awareness questionnaire. 14 minutes.

7023    *Diversity is . . . .* Offers a collection of insights into the place of diversity in our society from a wide range of perceptions. General Commission on Religion and Race, 1997. 15 minutes.

7024    *Images of Life/Visions of Hope.* Highlights four racial/ethnic local churches around the United States and their ministries to their communities. Produced by United Methodist Communications, 1986. 20 minutes.

7025    *Racism: The Church's Unfinished Agenda.* Highlights of National United Methodist Convocation on Racism, September 1987. Produced for the General Commission on Religion and Race by EcuFilm, 1987.

## J. Evangelical United Brethren Church

7026    *Uniting Conference of The Evangelical United Brethren Church, Johnstown, PA, 1946.* Archival film of conference that united the Evangelical Church and the United Brethren Church into the EUB Church. Produced by the General Commission on Archives & History, UMC, 1995.

## K. Global Ministries

*See also World Methodist Council videos, Section Z3.*

7027    *A Day of New Beginnings: 50 Years of Mission and Ministry through the Advance.* Celebrates 50 years of the Advance program. Produced by the General Board of Global Ministries, 1997. 24 minutes.

7028    *Love in Action: UMCOR 50 Years of Service.* Celebrates the 50th anniversary of the United Methodist Committee on Relief; shows past and present work. Produced by Norma J. Kehrberg for UMCOR, 1990. 60 minutes.

7029    *One World.* Video highlighting ecumenism through the World Council of Churches. Produced for the World Council of Churches, 1990.

7030    *The People Called Methodist.* Photographed in Australia, Singapore, Bolivia, Sierra Leone, Jerusalem, and the United States. Viewers see Methodists of many nationalities preaching, healing, and teaching in their own countries. Produced for the General Board of Global Ministries, 1991. 28 minutes. Available in Spanish and English.

7031    *To Flourish and to Grow.* Video describing the Interdenominational Cooperation Fund and how this United Methodist general fund supports the World and National Council of Churches and the

Consultation on Church Union. Produced by the General Commission on Christian Unity and Interreligious Concerns, 1990. 11 minutes.

7032 *Whom Shall I Send?* United Methodist missionaries in ministry through the Advance for Christ and His church. Produced by United Methodist Communications, 1995.

## L. Hispanic American Methodists

7033 *500 Years: Martyrdom and Hope.* Celebrates 500th anniversary of the discovery of Christopher Columbus' discovery of America, 1492. Produced by the Latin American Council of Churches, 1992.

7034 *Partners in Ministry: The Rio Grande Conference.* Celebrates the mission and ministry of the UMC's Hispanic conference in the desert Southwest. Leader's guide available. Produced by GBGM, 1995. 13 minutes.

7035 *We Belong to the Lord [Somos del Senor].* Celebrates the historic role of Hispanic people in the mission of The UMC. Produced by Linda Tafolla for UMCom, Nashville, 1992. Available through EcuFilm.

## M. Hoover, Theressa

7036 *Theressa Hoover: Through the Test of Time.* A tribute to Theressa Hoover, who served for 22 years as deputy general secretary of the Women's Division. Offers a vivid history of the organization and the women who created it. Produced for the Women's Division, General Board of Global Ministries, 1990. 21 minutes.

## N. Human Sexuality

7037 *AIDS: A Healing Ministry.* Scenes from a national UM consultation on AIDS in San Francisco, November 1988. Produced for the Health and Welfare Ministries Program Department of the General Board of Global Ministries, 1989. 32 minutes. Distributed by EcuFilm.

7038 *Casting Out Fear: Reconciling Ministries with Gay/Lesbian United Methodists.* A provocative, warm video portraying the painful stories of lesbian and gay men in the church and the struggles of congregations to be welcoming. Produced by the Reconciling Congregation Program of Affirmation, United Methodists for Gay and Lesbian Concerns, 1988. 38 minutes. Updated video promised in 1997.

7039 *Reconciling Congregation Program's 10th Anniversary.* Produced for the Reconciling Congregations Program, 1994.

7040 *Spread the Word: Teens Talk to Teens about AIDS.* Basic information on AIDS, with study guide. Produced by The Names Project, San Francisco, 1994. 27 minutes.

## O. Hymnody

7041  *Amazing Grace, with Bill Moyers.* A moving history of this timeless hymn. Features the Boys Choir of Harlem, Johnny Cash, Judy Collins, Jeremy Irons, Jessye Norman, Jean Ritchie, and Marion Williams. Produced by PBS, 1990. Available from Hymn Society in the US and Canada Book Service, Fort Worth, TX.

7042  *A Gift of Song.* Produced for the celebration of the bicentennial of Methodism in America, this video features five choirs, chosen by their respective denominations, singing selections that reflect the evolution of American hymn singing. Produced for the Pan Methodist Bicentennial Committee by United Methodist Communications, 1984. 30 minutes.

## P. Kelly, Leontine T.C.

7043  *Reflections on the Journey 1984-1988: Bishop Leontine T. C. Kelly.* Produced by California/Nevada Conference Historical Society, Berkeley, CA, 1988. Autobiographical reflections of The UMC's first woman of color to be elected bishop.

## Q. Lay Ministries

7044  *A Charge to Keep: An Introduction to The United Methodist Church.* Narrated by William Willimon, this video introduces new and prospective church members to The UMC by focusing on four elements identified as UM strengths: fellowship, worship, Christian education, and outreach. Produced by The United Methodist Publishing House, 1988. 30 minutes. Available from Cokesbury.

7045  *Living the Life! Congregations Answering Christ's Call to Be Advocates in Mission.* Highlights congregations in Wichita, KS, Des Moines, WA, and Fort Worth, TX. Produced jointly by the General Boards of Church and Society and Global Ministries, 1997. 45 minutes. Available from EcuFilm.

7046  *Vital Congregations/Faithful Disciples.* Introduces the United Methodist Bishops' 1990 pastoral letter on church growth by highlighting varieties of vital congregations. Produced by The United Methodist Publishing House, 1990. Available from Cokesbury.

7047  *Why I Am a United Methodist.* In seven segments, enhancing the seven chapters in his book, *Why I Am a United Methodist,* William Willimon leads viewers on a journey through The UMC. Willimon offers lively discussions of the history, theology, worship, and outreach of the denomination. Produced by The United Methodist Publishing House, 1990. 45 minutes. Available from Cokesbury.

7048  *Youthworks: Volunteers with Youth.* Details the Youthworks Program in the Louisville (KY) District, which matches adult volunteers with youths who are first-time juvenile offenders and have been referred to the program by the court. Produced by the General Board of Church and Society, 1997. 17 minutes.

## R. Local Church Historians/Committees on Records and History

7049 *Memory and Ministry: Caring for Your Church's Heritage.* Produced by the staff of the General Commission on Archives and History, 1996. Available from EcuFilm. 30 minutes.

## S. Matthews, Marjorie

7050 *Marjorie Matthews: Election to the Office of Bishop at the North Central Jurisdictional Conference, June 1980.* Archival film of election and consecration, 1980.

7051 *Recognizing the Ministry of Bishop Marjorie S. Matthews.* A celebration of the life and ministry of The UMC's first woman bishop. Part 1: selected video records of the 1980 North Central Jurisdictional Conference, interviews with Bishop Matthews, and remembrances; part 2: Dinner and Celebration, March 5, 1996, sponsored by GCOM. Produced by GCOM, 1996. 108 minutes.

## T. Native American Ministries

7052 *Faith That Endures: Bicentennial of the Oklahoma Indian Mission Conference.* Celebrates the past, present, and future of the Oklahoma Indian Mission Conference of The UMC, 1994. 14 minutes.

7053 *The Good Mind.* Compares Native American and Christian religious expressions and theology. Produced by The United Methodist Publishing House, 1983. 30 minutes. Leader's guide available. Order from Cokesbury.

7054 *Living the Dream: Native American Ministries.* Focuses on the Native American mission center in Greensboro, NC. With leader's guide. Produced by UMCom, 1994. 11 minutes.

## U. Social Justice

7055 *Charter for Racial Justice, A History.* Illustrates the history of the Women's Division work on the Charter for Racial Justice beginning in the 1940's. Includes study guide. Produced for United Methodist Women; available from GBGM Service Center, Cincinnati.

7056 *Claiming the Promise.* Three vignettes, which chronicle the story of three physically-challenged United Methodist pastors, dispel fears and doubts about the ability of persons with handicapping conditions to serve as church pastors. Produced by United Methodist Communications, 1991. 27 minutes.

7057　*The Community in Crisis: A Covenant Response.* Examines substance abuse confronting our communities; focuses on UM churches in the Washington, DC, area battling to reclaim young people and communities. Produced for the Bishops' Initiative on Drug Abuse, 1990.

7058　*In Defense of Creation.* Introduces the United Methodist Bishops' 1986 Pastoral Letter "In Defense of Creation: The Nuclear Crisis and the Pursuit of Peace." Produced by United Methodist Communications, 1986. 29 minutes.

7059　*Let Justice Flow.* Describes the work of the General Board of Church and Society. Produced for the General Board of Church and Society, 1995. 19 minutes.

7060　*More Than Words.* Profiles two congregations studying and acting on UMC Social Principles. Comes with study guide and leader's manual. Produced for the General Board of Church and Society, 1992. 20 minutes.

7061　*New Day: Theology and Addiction.* Produced by the Health and Welfare Ministries Program Department of the General Board of Global Ministries. 14 minutes.

7062　*The Retreat.* Introduces UMC Social Principles to young people. Produced for the General Board of Church and Society, 1992. 16 minutes.

7063　*The Revival of Hope.* Highlights what local churches in four Methodist denominations are doing to bring hope to their communities wracked by the drug crisis. Produced by the Pan-Methodist Coalition, 1991. Available from Cokesbury. 20 minutes.

7064　*The Social Principles.* Bishop James S. Thomas, chairperson of the Social Principles Study Commission 1968-1972, discusses biblical/theological foundations and answers frequently asked questions about the current Social Principles statement in The UMC Book of Discipline. Produced by The United Methodist Publishing House, 1990. 35 minutes.

7065　*Widening Circle.* Shows how churches can involve physically and mentally challenged people in the full life of their ministries. Includes a leader's guide by Susanne Paul. Produced by EcuFilm, 1994. 26 minutes.

7066　*Women and Children First: A Faith-Based Perspective on Reforming Welfare.* Produced for the Women's Division of the General Board of Global Ministries, 1995. 20 minutes.

## V. Walk to Emmaus

7067　*Walk to Emmaus: An Introduction.* Produced by the Upper Room, 1994. 14 minutes.

## W. Wesley, John

7068    *John Wesley.* A re-release of the J. Arthur Rank film classic made in England in 1954. Worcester, PA: Gateway Films, 1996. 77 minutes.

7069    *John Wesley: The Preacher.* Dramatic recreation of John Wesley preaching in the New Room, his famous chapel in Bristol, England. Produced by the BBC, 1981. 30 minutes.

7070    *John Wesley: The Proud Methodist.* Video biography of John Wesley privately produced for James Miller by Envisions, Fort Wayne, IN, 1988. 27 minutes.

7071    *The Man from Aldersgate: John Wesley.* Written by Brad L. Smith, featuring Roger Nelson. Produced by Gospel Film Productions, 1995. 110 minnutes.

7072    *Through Wesley's England.* Video tour follows the indefatigable Wesley to the key places he knew: Epworth, Oxford, London, Bristol, and other sites in the midlands and Yorkshire. Produced in England in 1988 by T.E. Dowley for the 250th anniversary of John Wesley's conversion. 30 minutes. Available from Cokesbury.

## X. Wesley, Susanna

7073    *Portrait of Susanna.* Dramatic presentation of Susanna Wesley in an "Evening with" format. Produced by the Continuing Theological Education Department of Drew University Theological School, 1982. 35 minutes.

## Y. Wilberforce, William

7074    *William Wilberforce, 1759-1833.* British aristocrat and Anglican evangelical who devoted his energy to the task of abolishing slavery in the British Empire. Leader's guide produced by Kenneth Curtis. Produced by Gateway Films, 1992. 35 minutes.

## Z1. Willard, Frances

7075    *Frances Willard.* The story of her life and work. Produced by the Continuing Theological Education Department of Drew University Theological School, 1984. 30 minutes.

## Z2. Women

*See also videos of individual women listed above: Theressa Hoover, Leontine Kelly, Marjorie Matthews, Frances Willard, and Susanna Wesley.*

7076    *Ask Before You Hug.* Tackles sexual harassment. Produced for the General Commission on Status and Role of Women, 1996. 38 minutes.

7077    *The Deaconess Story.* This well-researched video documentary explores the religious aspirations of the first generation of women who became Methodist deaconesses (1890's). Using authentic photographs, music composed by participants in the movement, and personal recollections of women who remembered the early days, *The Deaconess Story* captures the spirit, the substance, and the significance to women's history of this unique Protestant sisterhood. Privately produced in 1983 by Mary Agnes Dougherty and History Media, 909 Carmel Ave., Albany, CA 94706. 12 minutes.

7078    *A Lost History: 200 Years of Women in Methodism.* Interview format featuring Frances Willard, Anna Shaw, Harriet Tubman, Mary Bethune, and others. Produced by NBC News and the National Council of Churches, 1985. 60 minutes.

7079    *A Message to United Methodist Women.* An informational video concerning the ecumenical "Re-imagining Conference," Minneapolis, November 4-7, 1993, marking the mid-point in the "Ecumenical Decade: Churches in Solidarity with Women." Produced by the Women's Division of the General Board of Global Ministries, 1993.

7080    *A Tale of Two Genders.* Produced by the Southern New Jersey Commission on the Status and Role of Women, 1996.

7081    *UMW: Growing in Mission.* Looks at United Methodist Women, its history, concerns, and programs. Produced for UMW by UMCom, 1994. 14 minutes.

7082    *Wellspring of Hope: United Methodist Clergywomen's Consultation, 1987.* Evanston: General Commission on the Status and Role of Women, 1987

7083    *Women Called to Ministry.* Introduces the biblical and theological understandings of the ordination of women, sketches the history of clergywomen in the United Methodist tradition, and explores the current experience of local churches and clergywomen as they share in ministry. Produced by the Division of Ordained Ministry, General Board of Higher Education and Ministry, 1986. 30 minutes.

## Z3. World Methodist Council

7084    *People Called Methodists.* Produced by the Evangelism Committee of the World Methodist Council. 28 minutes.

7085    *To Live to God.* Introduction to the World Methodist Council and the World Methodist Museum, Lake Junaluska, NC. Produced by the World Methodist Council, 1985. 25 minutes.

7086    *World Methodist Council: "One People in All the World."* Produced by the World Methodist Council, 1996.

# PART VIII:
# DIRECTORY OF PRINCIPAL
# SUPPLIERS

*For Methodist publishers outside the United States and the United Kingdom, see 2013 and Part VI, Section 10. For out-of-print Methodist books, see the book dealers listed below.*

8001  Abingdon Press/The United Methodist Publishing House
      Customer Service Department
      201 Eighth Avenue, South
      P.O. Box 801
      Nashville, TN 37202-0801
      Phone: 1-800-251-3320 /FAX 1-800-836-7802

8002  Cokesbury Mail Order Center
      201 Eighth Avenue, South
      P.O. Box 801
      Nashville, TN 37203-0801
      Phone: 1-800-672-1789 /FAX 1-800-672-1789

8003  Discipleship Resources Distribution Center
      P.O. Box 6996
      Alpharetta, GA 30239-6996
      Phone: 1-800-685-4370 /FAX 1-770-442-9742
      Online: www.discipleshipresources.org.

8004  EcuFilm
      810 12th Avenue, South
      Nashville, TN 37203-4744
      Phone: 1-800-251-4091

8005  Epworth Press (England)
      c/o Trinity Press International
      P.O. Box 851
      Valley Forge, PA 19482-0851
      Phone: 1-800-421-8874

8006    General Board of Church and Society
Service Center
100 Maryland Avenue, NE
Washington, DC 20002
Phone: 1-800-967-0880

8007    General Board of Global Ministries
Service Center
7820 Reading Road
Cincinnati, OH 45222-1800
Phone: 1-800-305-9857
FAX 1-513-761-3722

*Kingswood Books, see Abingdon Press*

8008    Methodist Publishing House (England)
20 Ivatt Way
Peterborough
ENGLAND PE3 7PG
Phone (from US): 011-44-733-332202

*The United Methodist Publishing House, see Cokesbury*

8009    The Upper Room
Customer Services
P.O. Box 189
Nashville, TN 37202-0189
Phone: 1-800-972-0433


## Out-of-Print Sources

8010    Gage Postal Books
P.O. Box 105
Westcliff-on-Sea
Essex SS0 8EQ
ENGLAND
Phone (from US): 011-44-1702-715133

8011    Charles A. Green
P.O. Box 6095
Philadelphia, PA 19114-0695
Phone:1-215-824-1425

8012     Noah's Ark Book Attic
        Stony Point, Route 2
        Greenwood, SC 29646
        Phone: 1-803-374-3013

8013     E. Alan Rose, Bookseller
        26 Roe Cross Green
        Mottram
        Hyde, Cheshire SK14-6LP
        ENGLAND
        Phone (from US:) 011-1457-763485

8014     Phyllis Tholin Books (women's studies only)
        824 Ridge Terrace
        Evanston, IL 60201
        Phone: 1-312-475-1174

8015     George A. Zimmermann, Jr.
        19 Poinsetta Drive
        Deland, FL 32724
        Phone: 1-904-740-1821

# AUTHOR/EDITOR/COMPILER INDEX

*This Index lists the authors, editors, and compilers of the major works cited in these bibliographies by item number. It is intended primarily to serve as a guide for locating the works of a particular individual. For this reason, works produced by the boards, agencies, or organizations of the Church are not included in this Index, nor are works by John or Charles Wesley.*

Abbey, Merrill R. 3526
Abelove, Henry 3456
Abraham, William J. 3092, 3389, 4006
Acornley, John H. 3205
Airhart, Phyllis 3058
Albin, Thomas A. 4022
Albright, Raymond W. 3373
Alejandro, Dionisio Deista 3112
Ambler, R. W. 3039
Andersen, Arolo W. 3364
Andrews, Dee 3074, 3152
Ariarajah, S. Wesley 3295, 3296
Arias, Mortimer 3390, 3391
Asbury, Francis 3274, 4209

Babuscio, Jack 3457
Baert, Maria Luisa Santillan 3721
Baker, Frank 3021, 3075, 3578, 3711, 4018, 4030, 4035, 4044, 4061, 4093, 5010
Baker, Richard T. 3113
Baldwin, Lewis V. 3153
Barclay, Wade C. 3185, 3496
Bartelman, Frank 3216
Bartels, Francis L. 3098
Batsel, John 6002
Batsel, Lyda 6002

Batty, Margaret 4174
Baxter, Richard 3274
Beach, Waldo 4268
Beckerlegge, Oliver A. 4022, 4025, 4040
Behney, J. Bruce 3374, 3497, 5011
Benedict, Daniel T. 4232
Bennett, G. V. 3034
Berger, Teresa 3476
Berthrong, John H. 3297
Best, Thomas F. 3355
Bilhartz, Terry D. 3080
Birch, Bruce C. 4269
Black, Kathy 3546
Blair, Ralph 3458
Blankenship, Paul F. 3261
Blount, Emanuel Lee 3736
Bondi, Roberta C. 3579, 3580
Boozer, Jack S. 3215
Borgen, Ole E. 4223, 4233
Born, Ethel W. 3636
Bowden, Henry W. 3507
Bowen, Boone M. 4133
Bowen, Cawthon A. 3233
Bowmer, John C. 4173, 4183, 4256
Bowser, Beth A. 3415
Bowyer, O. Richard 3581
Boylan, Ann M. 3234

Bradley, David H. 3154
Brake, G. Thompson 3053
Brash, Alan A. 3459
Brash, William Bardsley 4120
Brasher, J. Lawrence 3436
Brewer, Earl D.C. 3547
Brevint, Daniel 4029
Breyfogel, Slyvanus C. 3375
Brown, Earl Kent 3622
Brown, Kenneth O. 3206
Bruce, Dickson D. 3207
Bruno-Jofre, Rosa del Carmen 3130
Bruton, Sheila 3613
Bucke, Emory S. 3056, 3059, 3452, 4103, 4113, 4114
Buckley, James M. 3645, 5012
Burdon, Adrian 3712
Burge, Janet 3623
Burgess, Joseph A. 3348
Burroughs, Jeremiah 3274
Burtner, Robert W. 4047
Buschart, W. David 4135
Butler, David 3335

Caldwell, Wayne E. 3437
Calhoun, Eugene Clayton 3099
Calkin, Homer L. 2001
Cameron, Richard M. 3548, 4132
Campbell, Barbara 3637
Campbell, Dennis M. 3068, 4007, 4179, 4194, 5013
Campbell, James T. 3100
Campbell, Ted A. 3022, 4062
Cannon, William R. 4063
Carder, Kenneth L. 4002, 4008, 4009, 4165
Carey, John J. 3460
Carwardine, Richard J. 3040, 3081, 3082
Cell, George C. 4064
Chai, Alice 3187
Chandler, Douglas R. 4147
Cherry, Conrad 4121
Chilcote, Paul W. 3624, 3625, 4166
Chiles, Robert E. 4047, 4094
Choy, Bong-Youn 3188
Church, Leslie F. 3023, 3024
Clapper, Gregory S. 3582, 4065
Clark, Elmer T. 3263
Clark, Jonathan 3025

Clarke, Adam 4210
Clement, Shirley F. 3399
Clendenin, Daniel B. 4135
Clifford, Alan C. 4066
Coan, Josephus R. 3101
Cobb, John B., Jr. 4010
Cochrane, James R. 3102
Cocksworth, Chistopher J. 4257
Coke, Thomas 4211
Cole, Charles E. 3416, 4122
Collins, Kenneth J. 4067
Colvin, Gwen 2012
Colwell, James 3114
Cone, James H. 3478
Conkin, Paul K. 4145
Coppedge, Allan 4068
Copway, George 3508
Costen, Melva W. 3718
Cracknell, Kenneth 3298
Cragg, Gerald R. 4042
Craig, James A. 5006
Crawford, Evans E. 3527
Crosby, Pamela J. 2006
Crouch, Timothy J. 3403
Crummey, David C. 3404
Culver, Dwight W. 3155
Cumbers, Frank H. 3538
Cuninggim, Merrimon 3417
Cunningham, John T. 4134
Curnock, Nehemiah 4034
Currie, Robert 3041
Curtis, Kenneth 7074
Curts, Lewis 3060, 5014
Cushman, Robert E. 4095, 4136, 4234

Daniels, George M. 3156
Davey, Cyril 3498
Davies, Horton 3713
Davies, Rubert E. 3009, 3010, 3054, 3627, 4041, 4159, 5010, 5015
Davison, Leslie 3217
Day, Albert E. 3405, 3583
Dayton, Donald W. 3218, 3381, 3438, 3439, 3440, 3666, 4131
Deats, Richard L. 3115
Deats, Paul 4096
Demaray, Donald E. 3618, 3619
Dent, Frank Lloyd 3418
Deschner, John 3262, 3355, 3356, 4069

*122*

*123*

Rogal, Samuel J. 3486
Rose, E. Alan 3047, 6001
Rowe, Kenneth E. 1006, 1009, 1013, 2003, 3057, 3061, 3069, 3070, 3198, 3237, 3246, 3302, 3512, 3676, 4084, 4171, 4214, 5024
Runyon, Daniel V. 3226
Runyon, Theodore H. 1019, 4016, 4085, 4110, 4274
Rupp, Gordon 3010, 3030, 5010
Russalesi, Steven D. 3352
Ruth, Lester W. 3729, 4248, 4261

Sackmann, Dieter 3717
Saliers, Don E. 3594, 3595, 3598
Samartha, S. J. 3295
Sanchez, Diana 3487
Sanders, Paul S. 4226, 4227, 4262
Sangster, Paul 3238
Sangster, William E. 4086
Sano, Roy I. 3368
Schilling, S. Paul 3488
Schisler, John Q. 3239
Schmidt, Jean Miller 1009, 1010, 3070, 3565, 3566, 3677
Schmidt, Martin 4087
Schneider, A. Gregory 3088, 3089, 3596, 4032
Schoenhals, G. Roger 4032
Scott, Leland 4113, 4114, 4115, 4116
Seamands, Stephen A. 4112
Seifert, Harvey 3567, 4284
Selen, Mats 3048
Sell, Alan P.F. 3324
Semmel, Bernard 3016
Semple, Neil 3071
Senior, Geoffrey R. 3127
Seymour, Jack 3240
Shank, David A. 3111
Shawchuck, Norman 3610, 3611
Sheils, W. J. 3036
Sherman, David 5033
Shin-Lee, Kyung-Lim 3128
Shipley, David C. 4117, 4118
Shockley, Grant S. 1015, 3178, 3241
Short, Roy H. 3148, 4221, 4222
Simpson, Matthew 2016
Sizer, Sandra 3489
Sledge, Robert Watson 3095
Sloan, Douglas 3425

Smith, Brad L. 7071
Smith, J. Warren 3738
Smith, Timothy L. 3451, 3452, 3453
Smith, Warren T. 3179, 3180
Snyder, Howard A. 3226, 4151, 4152, 4153
Spann, Howard Glen 3387
Spencer, Jon Michael 3490, 3491, 3534
Stacey, John 4088
Stanger, Frank Bateman 3409
Stanley, Susie C. 3678
Staples, Rob L. 4228
Starkey, Lycurgus M. 4089
Steinmetz, David C. 4193
Stellhorn, Paul A. 3211
Stephens, Peter 3149
Stevens, Abel 5034
Stevens, Thelma 3568, 3679
Stewart, Claryle Fielding, III 3597
Stoeffler, F. Ernest 4119
Stokes, Mack B. 3227
Stookey, Laurence H. 3730, 4249, 4263
Straughn, James Henry 3096
Strong, Douglas M. 3090
Strong, James 2015
Suzuki, Lester E. 3202
Swanson, Roger K. 3399
Sweet, Leonard I. 3388, 3542, 3680
Sweet, William W. 3072
Swift, Wesley F. 3017
Synan, Vinson 3228

Tabraham, Barrie W. 3018
Taggart, Norman E. 3019
Takaki, Ronald 3203
Tavard, George H. 3337, 3339
Taylor, David L. 3731
Telford, John 4035, 4161, 4162, 4163
Templin, J. Alton 4141
Thomas, Hilah F. 3433, 3660
Thomas, James S. 3181
Thomas, Norman E. 3108
Thomas, Paul W. 3442, 3454
Thompson, Bard 4146
Thompson, E.P. 3049
Thorne, Roger 3247
Thorsen, Donald A. 4017
Thumma, Scott L. 3547
Thurian, Max 3354
Thurston, Branston L. 4172

*127*

Tigert, John J. 5035
Tillard, J.M.R. 3337
Tinker, George 3520
Tractenberg, Alan 5036
Trickett, David 3598
Trickett, Kenneth 3477
Tripp, David 3598, 3717
Troeger, Thomas H. 3527
Tucker, Karen B. Westerfield 3248, 3710, 3715, 3732
Tuell, Jack M. 1022, 3315, 5008
Turner, John Munsey 3007, 3008, 3020, 3055
Tuttle, Lee F. 3363
Tuttle, Robert G., Jr. 3229, 3400, 4090
Tyson, John R. 4021, 4091

Uminowicz, Glenn 3212

Valentine, Simon Ross 3031
Valenze, Deborah Mary 3634
Valin, Clyde E. Van 3696
Vergara, Alex R. 3129
Vernon, Walter N. 3540
Vickers, John A. 2004, 3506, 6007
Vischer, Lukas 3331
Vogel, Dwight 3599

Wade, William N. 3410, 3411, 3733
Wagner, James K. 3405
Wainwright, Geoffrey 3268, 3269, 3312, 3321, 3326, 3327, 3337, 3340, 3341, 3357, 3734, 4029, 4264, 4266
Wakefield, Gordon 3600, 3601
Walker, Clarence E. 3182
Walls, Francine E. 3455
Walls, William J. 3183
Walsh, John D. 3032, 3033, 3034, 3035, 3036, 3037, 3038, 3569
Waltz, Alan K. 2008

Wansbrough, Charles E. 5037
Ward, Alfred Dudley 3570
Ward, W. Reginald 3035, 4034, 4043
Wardin, Albert W., Jr. 3151
Warren, James I. 3492
Warren, William F. 3646
Warrick, Susan E. 2005, 2009
Washburn, Paul 3097
Watley, William D. 3270
Watson, David L. 3255, 3256, 3257, 3258
Watson, Phillip S. 4051
Watson, Richard 3477
Watts, Michael R. 3050
Wearmouth, Robert F. 3051
Weiss, Ellen B. 3213
Werner, Julia S. 3052
Wesley, Susanna 3604, 3621
Weyer, Michel 4143
Whaling, Frank 3603, 3606, 4052
White, James F. 3249, 3250, 3251, 3252, 3702, 3735, 4230
White, Susan J. 3252, 3716
Whyman, Henry C. 3369, 3370
Wilkes, Arthur 3214
Will, Herman 3524
Willard, Frances 3646, 3683
Williams, Dorothy L. 3461
Williams, Gilbert A. 3184
Williams, William H. 3078, 3079
Willimon, William H. 4254, 4255, 4267, 4275
Wilmore, G. S. 3161
Wilson, Robert L. 3525
Wimberly, Anne S. 3371
Wogaman, J. Philip 4285, 4286
Woo, Wesley S. 3204

Yoder, Don 3493
Young, Carlton R. 3494, 3495, 4030
Yrigoyen, Charles 2005, 2009, 4092